It's All About Energy
Adventures in Expanded Reality

Beverly Crane, PhD.

Blue Sun Studio, Inc.

It's All About Energy: Adventures in Expanded Reality
by Beverly Crane, PhD.

Website: http://www.transformationalexpansion.com/

Copyright © 2017 by Beverly Crane, PhD.
Publisher: Blue Sun Studio, Inc., Las Vegas NV

Cover and Interior Design: Blue Sun Studio, Inc.
Cover Background Image by: Beverly Crane

Notice of Rights
All rights reserved. No part of this book may be reproduced or transmitted in any form by any means, electronic, mechanical, photocopying, recording, or otherwise, without the prior written permission of the publisher.

ISBN: 978-0-9991520-4-1

Dedication

I would like to dedicate the book to all my students and clients over the last 25 years, who, through their interest, challenges, questions and curiosity, are the real forces behind my work. It was my interaction with them that prompted me to question and explore further, and ignited my passion for putting this all on paper. I am profoundly grateful to each and every one of them.

Contents

Prologue 1
Section One: It's All About Energy 5
   Chapter 1-Walking Between the Realms 7
   Chapter 2-An Updated World View 11
   Chapter 3-New Rules 14
   Chapter 4-A Different Way of Seeing 21
   Chapter 5-Energy and Consciousness 28
Section Two: Energy and You 33
   Chapter 6-Sensing Energy 35
   Chapter 7-Three Kinds of Feelings 43
   Chapter 8-Using Energy Senses in Choice 48
   Chapter 9-Your Personal Energy Field 53
   Chapter 10-Energetic Communication 60
Section Three: The Importance of Choice 65
   Chapter 11-Consciousness and Synchronicity ... 67
   Chapter 12-Choosing Your Expectations 74
   Chapter 13-The Secret of Happiness 80
   Chapter 14-Floating Potentials 86
   Chapter 15-Change vs. Transformation 93
Section Four: Understanding Duality 99
   Chapter 16-On the Necessity of Duality 101
   Chapter 17-Darkness and Light 105
   Chapter 18-The Nature of Evil 110
   Chapter 19-The Law of Reaction 115
Section Five: Relationships With Others 121
   Chapter 20-Energy Stealing 123

Chapter 21-The Origin of Vampires.................. 130
Chapter 22-Energetic Abuse................... 134
Chapter 23-Protecting Yourself 142
Chapter 24-Empathy and Anxiety...................... 148
Chapter 25-The Energy of Grievance................ 153
Chapter 26-Whining With Awareness 159
Chapter 27-Everyday Blessings........................... 163

Section Six: Relationship With Self 167
Chapter 28-Daring to Love Yourself.................. 169
Chapter 29-How to Love Yourself 101 174
Chapter 30-Transforming the Inner Critic...... 178
Chapter 31-Waves of Our Lives 182
Chapter 32-What is True Love?........................... 188

Section Seven: Soul Dynamics 193
Chapter 33-Energy Dimension Helpers............ 195
Chapter 34-Getting to Know Your Soul...........200
Chapter 35-Soul Language 204
Chapter 36-Connecting With the Soul 211
Chapter 37-Purpose vs. Passion............................ 216

Section Eight: The Aesthetic Imperative 221
Chapter 38-Creative Expression 223
Chapter 39-May You Walk in Beauty 228
Chapter 40-Lessons of Physical Creation..........233
Chapter 41-Limitation and Creativity...............237

Section Nine: Energy and Your Body.................. 241
Chapter 42-Synergy and Health...........................243
Chapter 43-Body Intelligence 248

Chapter 44-The Language of the Body 252
Chapter 45-Visualization and Healing.............. 258
Chapter 46-The Role of the Emotions 264
Chapter 47-Dialoguing With the Body 271

Section Ten: Some Practical Applications 277
Chapter 48-Garden Magic 279
Chapter 49-Working With Nature Spirits 282
Chapter 50-Soul to the Rescue 287
Chapter 51-Sam's Message 292
Chapter 52-Digital SoulSpeak 295

Section Eleven: The Larger World 299
Chapter 53-Political Chaos 301
Chapter 54-Recording Revolution 307
Chapter 55-Adjusting to Changing Energy 311
Chapter 56-What Does Freedom Mean? 316

Section Twelve: Wrapping It All Up 323
Chapter 57-Spiritual Perfection 325
Chapter 58-Integrating the Realms 330
Chapter 59-How to Enter the Flow 336
Chapter 60-A Time of Transformation 342

Appendix: Helpful Tools 347
Visualization #1 Running Energy 349
Visualization #2 Entering the Energy Dimension 353

About the Author 359

Prologue

As a child, I was always called "sensitive", which greatly puzzled me. I was not allergic to anything, nor did I object to being touched or hugged. So why was I "sensitive", and to what?

I did have what seemed to be unusual experiences (at least that's what adults told me) in that I sometimes seemed to know what others were feeling without any verbal communication and I could get dogs to do almost anything.

It took me many years to finally figure out the answer to these questions. I was sensitive to something most people don't recognize, but which nonetheless affects us all. I was sensitive to the subtle energy field that emanates from all physical things and also surrounds and connects us all.

It was this connection that allowed me to do things that could not be explained by physical laws of cause and effect, because the laws of energy are very different from those of matter.

Ever since that realization, I have been exploring this fascinating world of subtle energy, and, after many years of pursuing this objective, I can now say that I really do see the world multidimensionally.

I understand that we humans have two separate creative tools at our disposal, matter AND energy, each with its own set of rules and individual characteristics. Learning how to work with energy as well as matter, and to understand reality as an interplay between each of these realms, gives me a completely different perception of reality, a reality that can expand in all directions and is not dependent on time.

Even after these many years of learning however, I have only just begun the process. I am on the threshold looking out over a vast sea of potential and possibility. Seeing through the eyes of energy offers new insights every day, going in many directions I had never considered before.

Energy sensibility is not unique to me, however. It is accessible to everyone. It is much like playing the piano. Some people are born knowing how to do it. Others explore on their own and learn by experience. Yet others take lessons and become proficient. But everybody can learn well with guidance and a commitment to practice.

In this book, I hope to share my exploration and discovery of this new perception of reality, and also invite you to join me. I do this in the hope that it may offer the same understanding, comfort and sense of optimism for you as it does for me.

In these times when so many things are unsettled and chaotic, an expanded world-view is indeed a gift.

Section One
It's All About Energy

1
Walking Between the Realms

What is it like to live a life that can expand beyond the four dimensions of the physical world?

Living an expanded reality means walking between the realms – between the quantum and the physical, the spiritual and the temporal, the sacred and the ordinary, the magical and the mundane.

It means learning how to be equally comfortable in both realms, and how to choose one or the other when appropriate, or both at the same time according to our needs and desires.

How do we do this and what does it feel like?

Breathe in a couple of deep breaths and then take another. After the out breath, pause for a few seconds before breathing in again. Notice the stillness, the deep peace, the sacred silence of nothingness. Let yourself sink into this space between realms where your energy can reach out and touch everything in the universe.

Take some time to explore this emptiness, and discover within it the essence of all being, the doorway to the dreamtime, the mystical union of all opposites. Let yourself fill this space with your whole being, your body and also your soul, with the energy that both infuses the body and extends far beyond, touching, anointing and blessing everything.

In this place, we are deeply rooted in our physical bodies, but also energetically connected to all that is.

In this place, we are physical beings delighting in our ability to touch and feel and smell and hear and see and fully experience the beauty and even the ugliness around us.

In this place, we can feel into our true identity and reconnect with our souls and the divine wisdom of All That Is.

In this space, we can expand our energy field into many mysteries and magical places, as well as affect the contents of our reality by choosing a life of joy and passion.

This is the magic of energetic connection.

This is the feeling of sacred integration.

This is the secret of our humanity, that we are far more expansive than we thought.

Just as the body and soul are integrally a part of one another, so are the divine and human parts of ourselves. When we consciously enter the energy realm, we activate our quantum connections, our harmonic resonance with the rest of creation, and our ability to create a sacred space for ourselves whenever we choose.

In the past, we have separated these parts of ourselves because the physical world is a place of opposition and separation, of dualistic absolutes and attitudes like good vs. bad, black vs. white, sacred vs. profane. It is a place where conflict seemed necessary for right to overcome wrong. It is a place of limitation and stasis.

When we walk between the realms, opposites are not absolute but rather complementary. We can notice and observe, and even delight in apparent contradictions and differences while understanding the deeper harmony underneath.

Walking between realms means being able to see a cloud's silver lining as well as the dangers of getting to close to the sun. It means gaining a larger perspective that eliminates the need for conflict, and opens the doors to understanding and compassion.

When we walk between the realms, we discover that duality and limitation are spiritual helpers that bring us great gifts, creating access to wisdom and understanding that were not available before.

Walking between the realms means that we are

able to choose to be in either realm according to our needs, and to also choose both at the same time, to experience the sacred and the ordinary together in their mystical union.

This feeling, this place, this mystical connection with all creation, is available to us whenever we want. It is simply our intention that brings it about. We can choose to activate it whenever we think about it, and live within it even as we function in our physical world.

Walking between the realms is available to all of us right now. We have only to choose it.

2
An Updated World View

A worldview is how we look at, and understand reality. It provides us with the information we need to navigate in the world, to keep ourselves safe, and to seek success and happiness. It is so pervasive that we hardly ever think about it consciously. It just is! - very much like water to a fish.

Our current worldview in 21st century Western civilization, is still mostly based on our experience with physical matter and the Newtonian rules that govern it. These rules include cause and effect, the use of force as an instrument of change, the discrete separation of objects in space, and time as a constant that always runs in the same direction.

Although Einstein first proposed a reality based

on energy over one hundred years ago, even scientists puzzled about this new way of looking at things for many years thereafter. For everyone else, it made no difference at all until young people in the 1960s began to notice that human beings did, indeed, have energy attributes. We know this from the slang of that era. Phrases like "good vibes" and "bouncing off the walls" are metaphorical clues that energy awareness was beginning to break through to consciousness.

Today, at the dawn of the 21st century, most people agree that we can often pick up energy from other people or from spaces where intense energy has been focused. Many people have noticed feeling uncomfortable in a room where others have been fighting, and have experienced the energetic communication that allows them to know who is on the phone before even looking at the ID.

What is less commonly understood is the radical nature of a world where physical and energetic reality exist side by side. This is because the rules of physical reality and the rules of energetic reality are completely different, and in many cases totally opposite. This is why both awareness and understanding of the energy realm has been so slow to awaken.

The 21st century will be a time when we explore the profound changes in thinking that an awareness of the energy dimension brings. First, we will need to understand the unique attributes of energy and how different it is from matter.

Then we must learn the rules of this new realm and how to apply them effectively.

Eventually we will have to integrate our knowledge of energetic reality with that of physical reality so that we can navigate successfully in both.

And finally, we will discover how to make conscious choices about which rules are most appropriate to use in which circumstances.

Understanding the unique attributes of energy and the rules that govern it, helps solve many puzzles of human life. Events and circumstances that have always seemed inexplicable, now start to make perfect sense.

Learning to navigate the energy realm means moving into a more compassionate and loving relationship with ourselves and others, nurturing the ability to communicate consciously with both our physical bodies and our souls, learning to honor and respect the energy of plants, animals and the planet, and understanding how to manifest our greatest personal potentials.

This radical change is like telling a fish that it's now possible for him to live on land as well as in water, and that he has the potential to learn what he needs to make this happen. It may take him a while to master those skills, but the rewards are mind-boggling and beyond his wildest dreams.

And it's just around the corner.

3

New Rules

One of the most difficult aspects of exploring an expanded reality, is getting used to the idea that the rules of the physical world and the rules of the energy realm are not only different, but often completely opposite.

Even if we have never studied Newtonian physics we all understand the rules that govern the physical world because we have experienced them first hand all our lives.

1. Physical objects are discrete and contained, and occupy a set space that can be located and measured four dimensionally. In other words, I can tell you the position of any given object

by describing it in terms of its location in time and space, and I can predict the position of any object in motion by knowing the rate of force used in making it change positions.
2. Physical objects are separate from one another with a void in between. Most material objects have obvious physical boundaries that make them easily distinguishable from the space around them. This space between objects means that objects don't influence one another unless they are touching or otherwise physically, mechanically or electronically connected.
3. Time only goes in one direction, can be measured objectively, and is the same for everyone.
4. Stasis is the normal state of things and change happens only through cause and effect with the addition of some kind of force. The chair in your living room will stay in place unless something (you, an earthquake, etc.), exerts enough force to cause it to move.
5. Human consciousness observes a fixed reality that can be changed by human or natural forces, but is otherwise stable. We assume that we can observe reality objectively, and that it will remain the same during the observation process.

6. Force is understood as the engine of change in the physical world. When humans wish to create or rearrange physical objects, some kind of force is always required. In most cases, much work and effort is needed to manifest this change. Natural forces such as tornados and earthquakes also create change because of the great forces they possess.
7. The emphasis on absolute duality (bad vs good, for example) in the physical world makes it imperative for opposites to attract each other in order to affect some kind of balance. We see evidence of this in energy that comes from physical matter like electricity, where opposite poles attract, and also in human interaction where males and females are usually attracted to one another.
8. Physical resources are limited. There is only so much land, only so much water, only so much oil, only so much money, etc., etc., etc. The more I have, the less there is left for everyone else.
9. The mutual exchange of physical objects is a zero sum game. If I give you a pencil and you give me a pencil, neither of us gains or loses anything.

We live with these rules ingrained in our being, very much like a fish lives in water. The fish knows no other environment, and neither do we.

It's All About Energy: Adventures in Expanded Reality

Until now.

The rules of the energy dimension as they pertain to human beings, human interaction with others, and with the environment have not been fully understood yet. But we can correlate personal experience with information from quantum physics and other emerging scientific discoveries, and thus begin to make some fairly accurate assumptions about the rules that govern the energy realm.

1. Energy has no solid boundaries and can permeate objects. It is not discrete and cannot be located in time and space, nor measured in the same way physical objects can. It can best be imagined by thinking of a wave, with an ebb and flow of constant movement rather than a fixed object that can be mapped and easily located.

   Exact prediction is therefore not possible. With energy, we can only talk in terms of probabilities.

2. Energy connects rather than separates. Energy fields surround all physical objects and can extend outward for great distances, permeating everything and connecting us to everyone and everything. In quantum physics this phenomenon is called "quantum entanglement".

3. In the energy dimension time is not linear and may, in fact, be nonexistent, with all things

happening simultaneously. After entering the energy dimension, it is possible to speed time or slow it down consciously (to avoid being late for an important event, for example).

Dangerous or traumatic experiences may trigger this experience also, as in the middle of a car accident when time seems to slow down enough to allow you to figure out how to save yourself.

4. Although the physical world appears to be a place of stasis, the energetic world is completely the opposite. Energy is in constant motion with wave-like cycles, and probabilities changing every time anyone makes a choice different than what they would usually make.

   Energy's natural state is flow, and any obstruction to that flow creates problems in physical reality as well.

5. In the energetic dimension, choice and/or intention take the place of force, and synchronicity replaces cause and effect. In the world of energy, force is not only inappropriate, but counterproductive.

6. Intention takes the place of force in the energetic world because consciousness does have an effect on reality. We know from quantum physics that human consciousness plays a role in the outcome of experiments, which is why all drug testing today must be done with

double blind experiments where neither the patients nor the technicians know who is getting the placebo and who is getting the drug.

Human consciousness and human choice in particular, change probabilities on the energy level that then affect the outcome of what happens next in the physical world.

7. In the energy realm, it is not opposites that attract but rather similarities. This happens because of the underlying unity that comes about as a result of energy entrainment, which in turn causes the bonding of two harmonious or synchronized energy fields. Energy wants to be coherent, that is, in sync with all other energy around it.

8. Energy is not finite, but unlimited. We don't have to steal energy from others because we can generate our own through laughter, play, creative expression, healthy social interaction and loving ourselves. We can also just breathe it in whenever we need it.

   Energy is always available to create and play with. We learn how to access and use it by understanding and applying the vastly different rules that govern it.

9. Mutual energy exchange is not a zero sum game. If two people give each other an equal

amount of attention (energy), the energy generated multiplies exponentially, meaning that both get back far more than they gave out.

This does not mean the rules of the physical world are obsolete or unnecessary. We are physical beings as well as energetic beings. The rules of the physical realm are still necessary to keep us safe and to help us interact with our material surroundings.

Now we can begin to understand that these two realms can exist side by side in our lives if we are adventurous enough to open our perception to include both of them.

While learning and using the rules of the energy dimension may seem daunting, knowing when and under what circumstances they are most effective and appropriate, is perhaps an even greater challenge. The rewards are more than worth it.

4
A Different Way of Seeing

Because energy reality is so different from physical reality, expanding our perception means being open to seeing things differently.

This is especially important in today's world where things are changing very fast, and the chaotic energy of mass consciousness is affecting all of us. To make it even worse, as many of us wake up to the energy dimension, we also become more energy sensitive. We can feel the chaos, the pathos and the misery of others far more, and far deeper than ever before. It hurts to watch the news and/or be around friends or family members who are in constant drama. Living multidimensionally can be very difficult due to this added energetic empathy.

This is why it is important to learn how to "see" differently so that we can understand what's happening on a deeper level, and do not put situations or events into black and white boxes.

In the world of energy, nothing is black or white, even though these absolute opposites seem so distinct in the physical world. In the energy realm, there are natural cycles rather than permanent absolutes. These cycles are normal and healthy, helping energy flow, move, connect and expand.

Some days, for example, my mood is high. I feel joyous and expansive. I move out into the world and share my contagiously exuberant energy with everyone I meet and with everything I do.

On other days, my mood is low. I hibernate and move slowly. I know this is a time to refresh and replenish myself, to engage in self-reflection and quiet. One is not better than the other – both are needed.

When we "see" from an energy perspective, it is easier to deal with the anxiety and worry that come from the problems and responsibilities of life in the physical realm. A period of relative abundance will naturally be followed by a time of relative ebb. But that will again be followed by an increased flow.

And so it goes.

This principle operates on a larger scale as well. The "tragedy" of a newborn with a severe handicap can turn into the wonderful reunification of an extended family that comes together offering help. The excitement and joy of a college graduation then ebbs into the anxiety of unemployment, only to be followed eventually by the job of one's dreams. A colicky baby grows into a happy child, and a truculent teenager becomes a responsible adult.

Looking back on our own lives, we can probably remember many situations that first seemed tragic and horrible, which later turned out to be very fortuitous. We also may recall other events that seemed wonderful or miraculous at the time, then later proved to have a definite downside.

In each ebb, we think the flow will never return, but just like the sun, it always does, provided, of course, that we allow ourselves to "see" it.

Living a multidimensional life also requires us to change our perspectives depending on which realm we're operating in. Changing perspectives means getting out of our comfort zone and experiencing the world from a completely different set of rules and expectations.

Here are a few ways we can change our way of seeing in order to experience the world of energy.

1. In the energy realm, time is either non-existent, runs both ways, or can be slowed down or speeded up. Notice how time slows to a crawl when you're engaged in a boring task,

and then disappears completely when you are doing something you love. This experience is not an illusion. It's a result of the way you're managing your energy field at the time.

The next time you're late, try relaxing and releasing the anxiety that being late is producing. Raise the energy frequency you're operating in by entering the energy dimension (see #2 in Appendix). Don't look at your watch, just expect you will get there in time, and then see what happens.

2. In the energy realm, similarities attract, not opposites. This is why we get what we expect, not necessarily what we want. For example, when we feel abundant, are appreciative for what we have, and expect the best in the future, good things tend to come our way.

The next time you're in a bad mood, notice how many other unfortunate things seem to follow you around. When we are upset and angry, that unsettled dissonant energy attracts more of the same. If, on the other hand, you take a deep breath, calm down, and think about the important information that may be contained in whatever incident you are fuming about, you may be surprised at the insight you receive.

3. Physical objects are discrete, but energy is

not. Many different kinds of energy can occupy the same space, while specific energy can exist in many locations at the same time. Your energy can simultaneously be present in your body, surrounding your ailing mother, and accompanying your child to school.

When I was weaning my children, and they woke in the night crying for me, I knew they were not hungry but just wanted the comfort of my presence. From my bed, I sent my energy to them, wrapped it around them and hugged them close. Soon after they stopped crying and went peacefully back to sleep.

Your energy is yours to command, and it can be anywhere you choose for it to be.

4. Since like energy attracts like energy, we can be unconsciously influenced by those around us. Start to notice how your thoughts, feelings and moods change when you are with different people.

For example, being with one friend may make you feel lighthearted and joyful, while being with another weighs you down and makes you feel frustrated and responsible for their well-being. We are unconsciously affected by those around us far more than we think. As you become aware of the differences in other people's energy fields, you will "see" your relationship with them in an entirely new way.

5. Changing our perspective is difficult because in order to achieve that change we must consciously change our expectations. Sometimes it is easier to do this if we experience a change in physical perspective. This gives us a chance to experience what it feels like to "see" things from a different place.

6. When I was a child, I remember laying on my back and hanging my head off the bed so I could see the world as if it were upside down. What a difference! It was a whole new way of looking at things, and presented a world that in no way resembled what I was used to.

Here is an exercise to try.

We all generally experience the world from the height of an adult human. To get an idea of what a change in perspective might feel like, try seeing the world from a very low angle (like your small dog or toddler), or lay on your back and look straight up and pretend up is down.

With your smartphone or camera, take some photos from the ground straight on, or from a low angle looking up. Notice how different the world looks and how many interesting and beautiful things you find from that angle. Open yourself to any insights that might come as a result of seeing things from this different perspective.

This exercise can help us become consciously aware of all the things we are generally NOT seeing, (and not just from a low angle). It can broaden our ability to take in new information, provide many insights, and open us to experiences that we may have missed before because we assumed we knew what to expect.

When we try seeing the physical world from a new perspective, we open ourselves to allowing the energetic realm to reveal itself as well.

Remember that the laws of energy are different from the rules of the physical world, and we must learn to "see" differently in order to notice how energy affects our lives.

5
Energy and Consciousness

"Seeing" the world in terms of energy involves taking consciousness to a new level. The problem with the word "consciousness" is that it has two different meanings that are not usually distinguished.

The word "consciousness" is generally used to describe our mental perception of physical reality. This perception allows us to observe a situation, make choices based on what we perceive, and then relate that information to past experiences and our own survival.

The combination of our emotions, our mental ability and our physical response to pain and pleasure work together to ensure that painful or unpleasant sensations are treated one way and pleasant experiences are treated in another way.

When we become conscious of something that has hurt us in the past, we automatically, almost instinctually, seek to avoid whatever caused the pain. When confronted with something that has resulted in a pleasant experience, we seek to repeat the experience without even thinking much about it.

This kind of consciousness depends on current and past interactions with the physical world, and is meant to keep us safe and on the planet for as long as possible.

Since energy perception is not usually available to our physical senses, we need to bring our consciousness to a new level in order to begin interacting with the energy dimension. This new level is sometimes called "meta-consciousness" or being conscious of being conscious. Another word often used is "awareness" which refers to a level of observation that is beyond what is usually needed just for survival.

Awareness involves a number of higher order conscious functions, the first of which is personal reflection.

When we become conscious of being conscious, it allows us to achieve a certain level of distance from ourselves, which in turn facilitates the ability to be more objective about our own reactions and thoughts. The ability to move to this new level depends greatly on how honest we are willing to be with ourselves.

Being honest with ourselves enables us to observe our own behavior as if we were observing a third person, sharply reducing the need to defend and protect ourselves from criticism at all costs. We are also more able to manage our thoughts rather than to let them manage us. We don't take others' criticism personally, and can choose how to respond to internal criticism of ourselves.

We realize that we can choose what we think, but only if we first observe what we are thinking and make conscious choices about what it is that we are thinking about at any given time.

The objective distance from ourselves that comes from being conscious of being conscious, allows us to be more honest, not only with ourselves but with others as well. We can then see our own flaws more easily and thus develop compassion for ourselves, which in turn makes us more compassionate toward others.

We begin to see all humans as brothers and sisters in the great adventure of human existence, rather than putting people in categories of "us" and "them", "good" and "bad".

Once we have attained a certain level of self-reflection, it is much easier to use this new level of consciousness to work with the energy dimension. Self-reflection means that we are actively observing the world with the intention of seeing new things, and of having new elements, ideas and attitudes that were unconscious before, break through into conscious awareness.

Honesty and objectivity allow us to be much more adventurous and much less fearful and insecure.

Since we cannot see, hear, taste, touch or smell energy, we must look for it in the way it interacts with our physical body and our environment. In the same way that quantum physicists study invisible energetic elements like quarks and strings, we must study energy by observing not the thing itself, but the outcome of its interactions with the physical world.

Being conscious of being conscious gives us the mental tools needed for this task.

This kind of awareness is especially important in working with energy because this higher level of consciousness is the main factor in how we move and transform energy. Consequently, it is vital for us to be aware of where our *attention* is focused and what kind of *intentions* we set, since these two mental functions have great consequences in how energy will serve us.

Conscious awareness is our ticket to the energy realm. Choosing where we focus our attention and how we set our intentions will determine where the ride will take us.

Section Two

Energy and You

6
Sensing Energy

Developing conscious awareness, (or consciousness of being conscious), gives us the skills we need to explore non-physical realms. Awareness enables us to start noticing our energy senses and what they are trying to tell us.

While we're all familiar with our five physical senses, we also are born with the ability to sense energy. Often called the "Sixth Sense" and equated with intuition, this sense is really multiple senses that help us gather data from the energy realm, just like our physical senses gather data from the physical realm.

We all have the potential to sense energy even though many of us are not aware of it or are only now beginning to notice the energy around us. Because these abilities have generally not been acknowledged, and are even disparaged in our culture, we quickly learn to hide, disown or deny them in childhood so that they most often remain dormant and undeveloped as we grow into adults.

In order to cultivate and develop our energy senses, we must first acknowledge the realm from which they come. Most people agree that Einstein added a fourth dimension (time) to the other three that we are familiar with. What is less generally understood, is that for all practical purposes, he also added a fifth dimension, a dimension of energy.

Once we become aware of this fifth dimension and the fact that it exists side by side with the other four, confusion often sets in because we automatically expect that this dimension is governed by the same rules as the other four. We also expect that we should be able to explore the energy world with our five physical senses. This is also not possible.

Energy senses are different from physical senses even though most of them have physical sense analogies which help us understand them better.

There are six main energy senses; clairsentience, clairaudience, clairvoyance, clairalience, clairgustance and claircognizance, or "knowing".

Clairsentience is the energy sense that is most easily developed and the one that most people have already experienced. The ability to feel the hostility in a room is the early awakening of this sense. Clairsentience is the ability to feel energy, not just in your surroundings, but also the energy of other people, pets, trees, plants and even inanimate objects.

Developing this sense depends on your ability to connect deeply with people or things around you, that is, connect on an energy or quantum level by aligning your energy with that of others.

Connecting this way is easier if you first concentrate your own energy in your heart area until your chest grows warm and you feel the energy of compassion and gratitude spill out and seek to connect with everything around you.

There are many ways to "feel" energy. You can feel energy either with the hands, or sometimes with other parts of the body. A clairsentient healer will often feel a client's pain before the client describes it, or sometimes before the client is even aware of it. This clairsentient feeling can take the form of feeling the same form of pain in the same part of the body, for example, a stomach or headache which starts when the client enters the room and stops when he/she leaves. Or it can take the form of feeling the energy of the pain without really experiencing the pain personally.

Feeling energy with the hands is not usually as

dramatic and often results in feelings of tingling, warmth and movement.

You can also "feel" into the energy fields of other humans, disincarnate beings, plants, animals and even inanimate objects in order to receive information. This is a higher order skill and usually takes a while to develop.

The ability to perceive or see energy visually is called clairvoyance. It describes both the ability to see energy fields around people or objects with your physical eyes, as well as the ability to see distant or future happenings or important information with an "inner" or third eye.

This sense can be activated in 4D reality for some people, but also in one's imagination. In other words, it is often possible to see another's energy field by closing your eyes and letting energy come together and form images in your imagination.

Clairvoyance is often used to refer to being able to "see" into the future. But it is also possible to "feel" into the future with clairsentience. When you project yourself into a future event or possibility you can often feel the event taking place. If you feel a void instead, it tells you that the probability of the event happening is not good.

While this kind of feeling into the future is still called clairvoyance, it is really a clairsentient ability.

Clairaudience is the ability to hear energy vibration in the form of voices or tones that convey information. In its most subtle forms, clairaudience is often mistaken for talking to yourself. Clairaudience sometimes seems like a voice in your head, or your own voice, but in other cases people actually sense a voice outside of themselves right next to their ears.

Clairaudient information can also come straight from the energy dimension in the form of important tones, sounds, words, phrases or whole paragraphs. These less subtle forms can often be dramatic and sometimes involve sounds with unmistakable emotional information.

Clairgustance is the energetic taste sense. This sense is sometimes experienced by animal communicators when a pet wants its food changed.

Clairalience is the ability to smell energy. Smell is one of the ways a spirit guide or other disincarnate being may choose to make its presence known.

Often, one or more of these abilities are combined. For example, while sensing energy with the hands, a body worker may then receive spontaneous images relating to the kind of energy the hands are feeling and sometimes even the origin. She may at the same time also hear information in some form that further helps pinpoint the problem.

There is also a sixth kind of energy sensing which, for want of a better word, is simply called "knowing" or claircognizance. "Knowing" seems to be a very well developed form of intuition that goes beyond just sensing energy. It's as if there is a direct pipeline to infinite truth or wisdom that suddenly makes itself known.

"Knowing" may happen because the other five senses are well developed and thus can perhaps be understood as an instant combination of a number of senses to produce a whole. Or it can exist in individuals who have not developed any other abilities at all, and then becomes the sole way of gathering energetic information.

Claircognizance happens when something pops into your head that you know to be absolutely true even though you have no logical way of proving it, and even every logical reason to doubt the information you are getting.

"Knowing" has a certain energy of its own that is instantly recognizable and causes you to trust the information completely.

The first step in awakening your energy senses is to begin to experience your everyday world as a world filled with energy. The more aware you are of the reality of the energy fields of all things around you, the more you are likely to feel connected to that energy. And the more connected you are, the more you stimulate your energy senses.

The second step is to learn how to pull your own energy back to you and ground it. When you consciously connect to the ground you are tapping into the universal energy field via its concentration in the Earth.

Grounding your energy provides an anchor that helps structure energetic information into a form that we can access and understand. Without grounding our personal energy field is usually too distracted and scattered to be able to connect to the other energies around it.

The third step is to bring some or all of that grounded energy back up into your heart, which is the seat of our connections with other beings of all kind. When energy emanates from a compassionate heart, other beings feel comfortable letting us in and welcome the sharing of energy and information.

The fourth step is to be aware of, and take seriously, the subtle energy information you are being bombarded with at all times.

Compared to the physical stimuli we are used to, energy information seems ephemeral, that is, too subtle to be taken seriously. Ironically, energetic information is usually much more reliable than physical information. Our eyes and ears can be fooled, but our energy senses, once developed, are usually never wrong.

Awakening your energy senses takes practice and commitment. Although some people are obviously more talented than others, everyone has the ability to develop at least some of these skills. Very few people are gifted with all of them, and one or two will usually be more active than others.

Just like the physical senses where some people are visual learners while others are aural or kinesthetic learners, you will develop the energy senses that are most appropriate for you.

7
Three Kinds of Feelings

Although the more common and well-known term for claircognizance is simply "intuition", the way this word is used usually confuses claircognizance and clairsentience.

When talking about intuition we often use the words "feel" or "feeling". We ask ourselves, what is our intuitive feeling about something – or we try to "feel" into a situation in order to make a decision. The word "feeling" used in this context, is ambiguous because it has so many meanings.

We have physical feelings when we use our sense of touch. Our fingertips can feel texture, temperature and the density of physical objects. Therefore, we often use physical analogies to describe intuitive feelings (prickly, silky, rough, heavy) since we have no other words available to describe energetic sensations. Nonetheless, the word "feel" traditionally describes a physical sense.

Feelings are also emotional. Emotions are e-motions, or energy in motion, either pulling us toward positive experiences or repelling us away from negative ones. Emotional feelings always have an agenda – keeping us safe from pain or danger, or following the attraction of something pleasurable or beneficial.

But intuitive feeling is different from both physical and emotional "feeling".

It is also completely different from logic, which is perhaps why we use the word "feeling" in order to emphasize that intuition is somehow the opposite of reason. Since intuitive information is often exactly the antithesis of what reason or logic would suggest (although it doesn't have to be), it is easy to confuse emotional and intuitive information.

When seeking to develop intuitive abilities, it is important to distinguish between emotional and intuitive feelings.

Emotional feeling is dualistic in nature. We perceive something as either good for us, or bad for us, so whenever we have what we might think of as a positive or negative intuitive feeling, it is necessary to check if there are any other purely emotional reasons for this feeling.

It's All About Energy: Adventures in Expanded Reality

If, for example, my attractive stockbroker friend recommends a particular stock, I may have an exceptionally positive feeling about that stock, and think it's my intuition telling me to buy it immediately. In a situation like this, it's important to ask myself whether it's really an intuitive feeling about the stock itself, or an emotional attraction to the stockbroker.

If I buy a plane ticket to Hawaii and see on the ticket that the plane is a 777, I may begin to have negative feelings about the flight. Is this really my intuition telling me not to make the trip, or is it an unconscious emotional reaction to a recent news story about a 777 that crashed?

We often mistake emotional feelings for intuitive ones because they come on hard and fast with a huge emotional charge, seemingly out of nowhere. What else could they be other than intuitive?

Some years ago, I was traveling on an interstate and found myself close behind a large truck. All at once I had a sudden graphic vision of the truck slamming on the brakes, and my car careening into the underside, decapitating me!

At first I panicked, thinking this was an intuitive flash warning me of impending disaster.

After quickly searching my thoughts for a possible emotional cause, I recalled that years ago, I had an acquaintance die in just such an event. I realized that finding myself in similar circumstances had triggered unconscious connections to that tragedy. What I thought was an intuitive hit was a strong emotional reaction to an old memory triggered by my current situation.

I slowed down just in case, but the truck never slammed on its brakes. It was not intuition after all, thank goodness.

Confusing these two kinds of feelings is one of the reasons we grow to doubt our intuitive abilities. Intuition generally gives accurate information about something we had no way of knowing about otherwise. Emotional feeling bases its responses on prior experiences.

If I had continued to think my truck vision was intuition without discovering its emotional basis, I would have been confused by the experience. Although I was obviously grateful that my vision never materialized, not being able to tell the difference between emotional and intuitive feeling would have made me more likely to dismiss a true intuitive hit next time.

Mistaking emotional feeling for intuitive feeling creates self-doubt and prevents us from recognizing the energy of true intuition.

It is important to trust in our own innate ability to develop intuition. Like any other skill, it takes time and practice. Learning to separate emotional and intuitive feelings helps us gain confidence and learn what true intuition "feels" like.

After experiencing real "intuition" a number of times, we grow to recognize its energy and then can tell the difference just by the "feel" of it.

8
Using Energetic Senses in Choices

When you learn to experience everything as energy, it has profound effects on the way you live your life and the choices you make. Although logic and mental discernment are still helpful, you are now more concerned with your energy interactions, not only with people and other living things, but also with choices about where you go and what you do.

The internet and the wealth of information it provides can be an effective and efficient tool for making choices. But often this abundance causes our brains to overload and shut down when faced with so many opportunities.

Too many choices can often be worse than too few.

This is what happened to a friend when she and I were discussing choices for her upcoming overseas vacation. There were dozens of hotels for her to choose from, and many tools to help make that decision. There were hotel websites with lots of great photos. There was advertising and sites like TripAdvisor where you can see the comments of others.

She had so many choices and so much information that she was paralyzed and stuck. She was trying to use her mind to sort out all the information, but instead became confused and uncertain. This indecision was also leading to anxiety about whether it was possible to make the right choices at all.

When your mind is overloaded, you have another way to make choices. You can employ your energetic senses.

Instead of relying on advertising and TripAdvisor (it's often just the cranks who write in anyway), let the energy of the place speak to you. Read the description and look at the photos and imagine yourself being there.

Let yourself sink into the energy of the space, and forget about all the mental information about which is the best. Notice how your personal energy changes when you do this.

Do you feel uncomfortable and ill-at-ease, or do you feel inspired and energized?

Do you feel anxious and on edge, or does your energy feel harmonized and resonant with well-being?

The energy connection between you and the choice you are considering will give you the information you need.

After first experiencing mental paralysis, my friend had an entirely different reaction when she used her energetic senses to connect or "feel into" her hotel choices. Instead of mental overwhelm and confusion, she was able to quickly distinguish the hotels that meshed with her own personal energy field.

On her return, she happily confirmed that her choices were excellent and her trip extremely enjoyable.

You can also use this technique to optimize your work-flow during the day. When you find yourself in a position to organize your own workday, you will notice that sometimes work seems to go quite quickly with successful outcomes, and other times it proceeds slowly with great irritation and many roadblocks and distractions.

I find that when I outline the work I have to do in a day and then feel into the energy of each project or activity, I can easily choose which one feels right in the moment.

When I allow my energy senses to choose instead

of my mind, I have a much more enjoyable and successful workday. I also accomplish much more than when I use my mind to determine what I should do next.

I have no logical explanation as to why the energy of one project feels right at one time, and the energy of another project feels better at another time, but as long as I let my energetic proclivities direct my workday, I really enjoy my work.

Even mistakes or roadblocks are fewer, and when they do occur I am not irritated, but treat them as interesting challenges.

If, on the other hand, I allow my mind or a deadline to force me into a job that I really don't want to do at the time, I find myself getting annoyed and irritated at the least little thing. Consequently I become easily distracted and make more mistakes than I would otherwise. My creativity is stymied and blocked and I have difficulty getting anything done.

Even if it is an activity I normally enjoy, doing it when I'm "not up for it", takes away all the fun and turns it into drudgery.

Trusting your energy senses can also give insights into the future.

When you plan a vacation, and then start feeling uncomfortable about it for no good reason, you may be receiving important intuitive information. For me, feelings of unease about future events usually mean that they are probably not going to happen, or if they do, they will not be enjoyable.

Now when this happens, I pay attention and feel into other choices until I land on one that carries more positive energy.

It takes awareness to remember you have energetic senses.

It takes attention to use your energy senses to help make choices.

It takes intention to make the choice to trust your intuitive feelings.

Start small and then notice the results. You will be amazed at how much easier life becomes.

9

Your Personal Energy Field

The degree to which you become comfortable navigating the energy realm will depend on your ability to manage your personal energy field.

All physical objects have energy fields, but the human energy field is the most complex and interactive. Until you learn to consciously manage your energy field, it will manage you.

Your personal energy field is a priceless gift. Managing your field is even more important than managing your time or money, although the analogies can be insightful. When you fail to make conscious choices about how you manage your time, you never seem to have enough, you are always late, always behind schedule and never seem to get caught up. Life is much more difficult than it needs to be.

When you are not conscious of your energy field and how to manage it, you are constantly getting embroiled in relationship issues, are easily exhausted and drained by other people and circumstances, suffer excessive and unexplainable anxiety, and are at a loss about what to do about it. Life is much more difficult than it needs to be.

Unlike time, however, most people are not even aware that they have an energy field, let alone how to manage it.

First, what do we know about the human energy field?

Valerie Hunt, a researcher at UCLA spent 25 years studying the human energy field using advanced telemetry techniques developed by NASA.* Here are some of her findings.

While all material objects possess energy fields, the human energy field absorbs and gives out energy actively, that is, it interacts with, and therefore influences matter continuously, while the energy surrounding inert matter is much more passive.

The human energy field or aura can extend outward from the body for great distances during meditation, ecstasy or great happiness, or be retracted from fear, insecurity, and conscious intention.

Our energy fields interact with our environment

and other energy whether we are aware of it or not, meaning that we are far more influenced by energy, both our own and that of our environment, than we know.

Hunt also found that the human aura has a negative charge (negative as in electrical, not to be confused with the kind of chaotic, incoherent energy that feels bad).

Since like energy attracts like energy, we humans are most comfortable in places that also have a negative charge, like the seashore, rivers and lakes, mountains and waterfalls. The Santa Anna winds in California are composed of positive ions. Consequently, people are restless and irritable when these winds are blowing.

Energy fields also play an important role in health. Hunt discovered that changes in health registered in the energy field before people were aware there was a problem, and even before medical technology could detect an abnormality. This fact suggests that disease begins in the energy field and then progresses to the physical body if steps are not taken to alter the field first.

Most importantly, Hunt found that the human energy field changed with intention, and intention could also influence other surrounding fields.

This one finding alone, speaks to the great importance of learning to consciously manage our energy fields. Until we do, we are unconsciously being affected by other people and our environment, while at the same time affecting others in ways we may not understand.

In my experience, the majority of relationship issues have to do with complex and unconscious energy field entanglements.

Because we are unaware of our energy fields and the need to manage them, we unconsciously project our energy out into our environment without understanding the consequences of our actions. Our energy can then easily become entangled in all kinds of situations that feel uncomfortable. Because we are not aware of how to reclaim our energy, we are at a loss for why we feel uncomfortable and have no idea what to do about it.

The greatest obstacle to learning energy management is wrapping the mind around the fact that conscious attention, intention and imagination really do move and direct energy.

Your energy field is yours to command. You no longer have to be buffeted about by your own scattered energy or the unfocused, chaotic or coercive fields of other people. You no longer have to feel uncomfortable in certain spaces because of the intense energy you find there. You have only to use conscious intention to remedy the situation.

Basic energy management means being able to consciously reclaim your own personal energy by bringing it back to your body. This initial action is called "centering" because it is most useful to place your reclaimed energy in the center of your body or "Hara" which is located just a few inches below the naval.

This skill is one of the first things taught in martial arts because centering increases your strength and stability, and augments your self-confidence, mental acuity and intuitive ability.

When you become aware of energy entanglements, or when your own energy seems out of control as in panic attacks or anxiety, you can pull your energy back to you with conscious intention. When you are just learning, a little imagination and ritual helps too, for example taking some deep breaths and imagining your energy returning to you with your breath.

Once you have reclaimed your energy, it is possible to consciously move it to many other places depending on what your needs or desires are at the moment.

Why are these skills so important?

We often use the word "merge" when speaking of overlapping energy fields, because that's what energy fields do. Energy has no defined boundaries like physical objects do, so when you give your attention to another person, idea or situation, you often merge your energy completely, depending on how intense your focus.

The idea of "merging" sounds scary, and it is, because there is always the fear that you will get lost in that with which you merge, and not be able to get out. This is precisely the problem with our energy fields.

If you are reading this book, there is a great probability that you are a caring, compassionate person who longs to connect with others in a deep and meaningful way. It may feel disloyal or selfish to separate yourself energetically from those you care about. Yuliya Cohen has succinctly described this problem in her excellent book, *Energetic Boundaries*.

"This instinct to merge with another, to help them whatever the cost, can be very powerful. However, the energetic rule is that you can only allow yourself to merge with someone else inasmuch as you have mastered the ability to separate yourself from others. Only after you have learned to define yourself completely, learned where you begin and where you end, only when you have taken full ownership of your own space, can you merge completely with another person and not get lost. If you have not gathered yourself first, you will get too entangled in the other person's space, feel confused and uncomfortable, and then will find it difficult to back out and distance yourself from them. First, we need to practice the discipline of separating from others for the purpose of gathering ourselves into our own field to find out who we are. Only then can we truly merge with someone."^

Personal energy field management means learning how to affect that separation so that merging is a conscious choice, and separating is easily accomplished when the time is right.

Once you learn to reclaim your energy, you are then free to place it where it will help you the most. Energy is a tool that wants to serve you. Like any tool, you first have to learn how to use it.

While basic management skills are referenced many times in this book, more detailed instructions and tools can be found in chapters 58-59 and the Appendix.

Infinite Mind: The Science of Human Vibrations, by Valerie Hunt

^*Energetic Boundaries: a Paradigm for Effortless Healing,* by Yuliya Lerner Cohen, pp.71-72

10
Energetic Communication

Energetic senses not only allow you to gather information from your surroundings, they also are an important means of communication.

When you begin to develop your energetic senses, you activate the potential for telepathic contact, not only with other humans, plants and animals, but also with disincarnate beings like loved ones who have passed over, angels, masters and spirit guides.

As scary as this may sound, it is only a potential. This ability will develop only if you want it to and are ready for it. And even then, it will probably develop slowly and in only a few areas at a time.

Telepathic communication from other beings can come through any of the six energetic senses.

Which of these senses is used often depends on with whom you want to communicate. Clairgustance, for example, is rarely used in human to human communication, but may be important when communicating with an animal.

Clairsentience and clairalience are often used when a spiritual being wishes to make its presence known to you. You will feel a tingling or warmth in a certain part of your body, or smell a certain kind of smell that draws your attention and introduces the being who wants to communicate.

In my experience, the most often used energetic senses for communication are clairaudience, clairvoyance and claircognizance.

Since humans are most comfortable with spoken verbal communication, initial contacts may come in the form of a voice inside or outside of your head. This is what happened to me.

After I started developing my energetic senses, I became envious of my human mentors who had spirit guides. I really wanted one of my own, but hadn't the faintest idea how to go about getting one.

I did have a daily meditation practice, but as I practiced silently sitting in waiting, I never received anything significant. Inevitably I would get bored and start thinking about some other philosophical question that had been puzzling me for weeks.

One day, as I was thinking about this kind of

question, I heard a voice in my head that sounded very much like my own voice, giving me the answer to my question.

It was a really great answer too. It was so good that it made perfect sense and seemed to be something I knew all along (although I knew I hadn't known – after all I had been perplexed by it for weeks). This began to happen regularly. The voice would not answer personal questions, like "what should I do now", only philosophical questions. However, I still couldn't figure out where it was coming from. (I was really dense about this stuff back then).

A few months later, I was at a workshop and had a chance to ask one of my mentors about the voice – whether he thought it might be a spirit guide?

He just roared with laughter and asked, "What do you think?"

The next day in meditation I asked the voice if it was a spirit guide, and got a resounding "yes!" Then I asked for a name and was given one, and so started a wonderful relationship that lasted many years and proved invaluable to my own spiritual development.

As this relationship developed, I began to get claircognizant and clairvoyant communications as well.

My guide would download whole boatloads of information in one huge dump, without any verbal communication or linear sequence. Nonetheless, I would somehow be able to absorb all of it and understand with no problem.

On other occasions, he would provide visual symbolic information that held great amounts of important information. (See Chapter 22). Clairvoyant symbols and claircognizant "dumps" seem to be much more efficient means of communicating complex explanations and/or ideas than verbal language.

I have had many other spirit guides since then (spirit guides change and you grow and evolve), and have also been able to communicate telepathically with humans, pets, plants, elementals (fairies, plant devas, weather spirits), ascended masters and those who have passed over (although none in great number).

Energetic communication of any kind is not something to be entered into lightly. We have evolved certain rules of etiquette for human physical and verbal communication that promote privacy and safety. Energetic communication with other humans can leave us feeling exposed and vulnerable if there is not a high degree of trust and skill in energy management.

If you find other humans with whom you are able to communicate energetically, you may have to make some ground rules.

Communicating with those who have crossed over is problematic as well.

When a person first crosses over he or she may seek out an energy sensitive person in order to communicate last wishes or words of comfort to loved ones. This kind of contact is usually short lived, and relating those words to loved ones can be very healing and comforting.

After the person moves on out of the Earthly dimension however, it is best to leave them alone because they have lots to do. If a disembodied entity refuses to move on, you can encourage them to go by telling them it's time to move on, and then ignoring them (removing your energy).

On the other hand, energetic communication with pets, plants and elementals can bring joy to your life. It can provide a sense of being truly connected to everything around you and provide help in many daily tasks. Being in contact with spirit guides and ascended masters (those humans who have graduated from the Earth cycle) can greatly facilitate your spiritual growth.

Section Three

The Importance of Choice

11
Consciousness and Synchronicity

Normally we think of consciousness as simply our ability to observe the world around us. When we start to be aware of the energy dimension, consciousness takes on a new role, becoming not just a passive way to take in reality, but an active way to both perceive multiple dimensions, and to use this awareness to create the kind of reality we want to surround us.

This is because we direct energy with consciousness.

While physical creation depends on force of some kind, energetic creation depends on intention. Therefore, the choices we make in how we think greatly determine how our reality is fashioned.

This may seem hard to believe at first, but you've

probably experienced the energetic effect of your choices many times in your life. Noticing these effects is why developing consciousness beyond the normal passive variety is so crucial in venturing into expanded reality.

Consciousness here is not just noticing our surroundings, but actively looking for the interaction between what we think, what we intend, and what happens next.

When we begin to develop this kind of awareness, we almost inevitably start to notice meaningful coincidences in our lives. Carl Jung called this kind of "a causal connecting principle" synchronicity.

How can we explain it when we have a question and a book falls off the shelf and opens to just the right answer?

Is it magic when we desperately need to attend a conference we can't afford, only to unexpectedly receive a tax refund just in time to register?

Synchronicity is an amazing and elusive concept.

Many of us have experienced it, and want to consider it real, but it just doesn't make sense from our knowledge of, and experience with, the physical world. After all, change in the physical world happens through cause and effect and the use of force. Meaningful coincidences or synchronicities seem to have no cause and effect associated with them other than human need or intention, and force is nowhere to be found.

In the quantum world however, consciousness does affect reality.

How does this happen?

Physicists really don't know for sure, but recently some in the scientific world are beginning to ask this question, and their theories give some interesting clues in the understanding of this puzzling phenomenon.

Most speculation revolves around quantum entanglement, which refers to the subatomic connection of everything to everything else. Specifically, scientists have found that particles that have been entangled energetically remain connected even after being separated in the physical world.

Einstein called quantum entanglement "Spooky action at a distance" and didn't believe it even though his theories predicted it.

Eventually however, physicists agreed that quantum entanglement is a fact, at least on the subatomic level. And today there seems to be growing agreement that quantum entanglement may be present in the macro (large object) world as well. It could well explain how fish school and birds flock, for example.

Now scientists are beginning to ask how consciousness may or may not affect entanglement, and why its effects are well documented in the subatomic world, but less obvious in the world of plants, animals and humans.

One important factor in these speculations is the role of *coherence.*

In physics, coherence means the matching, synchronization or entrainment of waves of energy.

When this happens, there is nothing out of phase and everything is working in harmony.

In the physical body, for example, coherence would mean that all physical, emotional, mental and spiritual energy systems are working in harmony and perfectly entrained, all working for the good of the whole. In this case, coherence would mean perfect health.

When an energy system is coherent within itself, it also has the capacity to link or connect energetically and become entrained with the energy of everything around it. Internal coherence begets external coherence, so to speak.

Quantum entanglement is easier and more possible on a subatomic level because the reduced complexity of smaller, simpler systems also reduces the chance that this innate coherence will be disrupted or knocked out of phase. The more complex and larger the system, the more chance that both internal and external coherence will be disrupted, and then the quantum or energetic connection is broken.

Although this is now just speculation among scientists, it begins to make sense when we apply it to what we know and have experienced in our own lives. The theory of energetic coherence may help us understand many mysterious phenomena that don't otherwise make sense.

In the human energy system, for example, a sense of coherence seems to be triggered in states of meditation, joy and ecstasy, artistic creation, play, love, and feelings of deep gratitude. These states are also when we are most likely to access our intuition, connect energetically to other people, pets or a higher source, or have healing effects on our own bodies or those of others. Successful energy healers have been found to have energy fields entrained with both the energy fields of their clients and the energy frequencies of Earth.

It could also be that choosing to be in a state of coherence triggers a quantum entanglement-like connection which influences future probabilities, in other words, *synchronicity.*

Setting an intention while in a state of coherence creates a new energetic field linking that intention with all probabilities needed for that intention to manifest, while at the same time, separating out all the rest. In other words, the process of synchronicity is set into motion when a choice is made from a state of coherence with that choice. This means that all human energetic systems (physical, emotional, mental and spiritual) must be in total agreement with the choice with no internal friction or external distractions.

This is why just setting an intention will not necessarily guarantee the desired result (as we all know so well). Anything that disrupts the internal coherence of the human making the choice, or the external connections to the probabilities necessary for the choice to manifest, can also interrupt the coherence between the human being and the entangled probabilities poised to bring the intention to physical fruition.

What are these possible disruptions? Here are just a few.

1. Internal doubt that the process really works.
2. Lack of clarity about what is being chosen or intended.
3. Subconscious fears and conflicts.
4. Extraneous stress and worry not related to the particular intention.
5. Effects of mass consciousness.
6. The soul's knowledge that the intention is not in the best interest of the person or the rest of creation.

The list could go on and on. We don't need to think hard to find examples – just examine our own experiences.

But anything we can do to increase our coherence with what we intend will encourage the energetic connections (synchronicity) needed to bring forth the intention.

Here are some suggestions as to how to increase coherence with your intentions.

1. Learn how to access the energy dimension and enter a state of coherence, also called "flow".
2. Trust yourself and your ability to use synchronicity effectively,
3. Gain as much clarity about your choices as

possible before you make them in order to be sure there are no internal or external conflicts about the intention
4. Experience the results fully in your imagination (see them, taste them, touch them, smell them, hear them). This entrains your physical being with the choice as well as your mental intention.
5. Let go of worry and stress of any kind,
6. Experience your intention as if it has already manifested.

Coherence also could be why spiritual work (attaining internal and external coherence) demands a certain amount of quiet, alone time. The more distractions and busyness in our lives, the more chance for the disruptions and distractions that break us away from the underlying energetic connection that is our birthright.

The real lesson, however, is the role of choice.

We can choose to be separate, and sometimes that is appropriate, and sometimes more than appropriate, and absolutely necessary. But we can also choose to connect, knowing that coherent energetic connections are what enables synchronicity. And when we do, manifestation and all the magical connections of the energy realm are at our fingertips.

12

Choosing Your Expectations

With all the drama in the world, it's hard not to expect the worst when it comes to our own lives as well. Especially at night, when sleep won't come, those negative thoughts just won't leave our brains alone.

After all, on the physical plane, our expectations are shaped by past experience. This is normal and part of how we learn to protect ourselves and control our environment.

If I burn my hand on a hot stove, I learn to avoid touching hot stoves in the future. With so much chaos and destruction in the news every day, it is hard not to expect that we might also be affected by all that's going on.

But expectation is a funny thing.

In the late 1960's Robert Rosenthal, a Social Psychologist at Harvard, discovered that the expectations of teachers could change even something as immutable as the IQ of their students.* If teachers were told that certain randomly selected students had higher IQs than other students, IQ tests the next year showed the IQs of these students had improved significantly (along with their grades).

"The Expectancy Effect" (as it was later called), shows us that we literally get what we expect.

While this seems counterintuitive based on our experiences in the physical realm, expectations are not physical, and when not used expressly to keep us safe in the physical world, they can be very limiting. Expectations are energy, and as such, they exist in the energy dimension and obey energetic rules.

One of the primary differences between the rules of the energy dimension and the rules of the physical dimension is what attracts what. In the physical dimension opposites attract. In the energy dimension, similarities attract.

This means that expecting negative things to happen will tend to draw those things to you, while expecting positive things will have the opposite effect. No matter what is happening around you, it doesn't need to affect you.

It's hard to change our expectations when most

of our past experiences can be logically explained by the simple cause and effect rules of the physical world. But if you think harder about your whole life, you can probably remember incidents where some other law appeared to be working.

Have you ever had a tooth hurt like crazy and then have the pain completely disappear after you decide to find a new dentist?

Do you remember all those times when your computer went haywire until you shut it down, did something else, and then came back to find it had fixed itself?

And what about that time (or times) when you had a "near miss", a car (or plane) accident where you really should have been dead?

It's so easy to dismiss and forget about these important incidents in our lives because they didn't make sense at the time. Even though the outcome was positive, we purge the memory from our brains. If we can remember some of these incidents, how many others have we forgotten? When things don't fit into our predetermined structures of understanding, we are quick to consign them to the garbage can.

Once we realize that there are two sets of laws working simultaneously side by side in our world, we can not only begin to understand these happenings, but start to anticipate more. If these kinds of things could happen in the past, then they can certainly happen again. Maybe my computer's hard drive really is shot, but maybe not. Maybe it's just trying to tell me to take a break.

Instead of dwelling on cause and effect in the physical realm, think instead about the way things happen in the energy realm, that is, with intention and synchronicity. You set the intention, generate coherence, and energetic laws take care of the rest (synchronicity).

But even intention can be limiting if it is too detailed and circumscribed. Be clear about the essence and then let the details go. In fact, the best expectations are no specific expectations at all. That way we are open to all potentials and possibilities. If we expect the unexpected, we allow the universe to work for us, to select wonderful events and outcomes that we might never even dream of.

In this way, we enlarge and expand the possibilities and potentials available to us. We are no longer caught in the limiting web of the physical, but can engage as well with the energetic dimension and all its magic, richness and possibility.

This is why people with a positive outlook always seem to "have all the luck", and people with negative outlooks always seem to have a cloud over their heads, with one bad thing following another. It's a good bet that both of these kinds of people originally had many of the same experiences, it's just they chose to look at them differently – the proverbial glass half full rather than glass half empty.

Having an optimistic outlook will ultimately affect not only you, but those around you. Positive energy vibrates at a higher frequency (generates more coherence) and will lift lower vibrations up to meet it, (but only if you resist the urge to let your energy fall in the presence of others' negative thinking).

It is also important to remember that we are ultimately responsible only for ourselves. That is, no matter how much we love others, we cannot and should not try to control their thoughts and/or actions, or blame ourselves if others get into trouble.

While our positive and compassionate energy will almost always be helpful to those around us, it may not result in what we might consider the best possible outcome. Each of us is responsible for our own choices.

In the case of others, as in our own lives, it is important to realize that even what appears to be a negative event, can turn out to be positive, but only if we expect an ultimate positive outcome and look for it. Sometimes the most beneficial outcomes are the results of what at first seem to be disasters.

The next time you fear the worst because that's "what happened last time", or because "it happened to someone else", or because "it's only logical", remember that it doesn't necessarily have to be that way. Living in a multidimensional reality means realizing that physical laws are not the only ones operating here on Earth. It also means stepping back and beginning to view things from a higher, energy perspective, where all things move together toward our next highest good.

*Robert Rosenthal and Lenore Jacobson, *Pygmalion in the Classroom: Teacher Expectation and Pupils' Intellectual Development.* (reprinted May 4, 2003)

13

The Secret of Happiness

Much has been made about happiness lately. There are lists of the countries with the happiest citizens. There are lots of studies and research about what factors bring about happiness. There are books that pull together all this information. But most of these sources leave out the most important fact about being happy.

Happiness is not a condition. Happiness is a choice.

When we understand how our choices affect the energy around us, we also begin to appreciate how important it is to make all choices conscious ones.

It is so easy to think that happiness depends on external conditions – whether we are financially secure, whether we and our loved ones are healthy and whole, whether we are fulfilled and "successful" in our jobs or careers, and/or whether we have loving friends and family who support us.

The truth is that most of us will never have every one of these things – especially all of these things at one time. And even if we do manage to acquire all of them at once, the situation will almost never stay that way. We will always have problems of one kind or another. They are part of being human.

Happiness is much more attainable if we change our attitude about problems.

Setbacks, obstacles and difficulties are not indications of failure or character defects. Problems are challenges and opportunities that expand our potential, stimulate our creativity, unleash our wisdom, and, in general, make life much more interesting.

Even in the midst of chaos, insecurity and grief, we can still choose to be happy. We can do this by enjoying and appreciating being physical and being human. Happiness can be found in simple, sensual experiences like:

The velvet fur of your purring cat,
The soft grass under your bare feet,
The kiss of a child, spouse or best friend,
The sun on your back,
The sound of a hearty laugh,

And the ability to cry and feel deep emotions.

After caring for a seriously ill loved one for many months, I have come to understand how it is possible to be happy even in conditions that others consider hopeless or tragic. Worrying about whether a loved one will live or die is certainly stressful and anxiety provoking, especially when you have no control over the outcome.

But I realize that I am in a situation that almost all of us must face eventually (unless we die first).

If we live long enough, we will inevitably find ourselves on one side or the other, either in ill health ourselves or caring for a sick loved one, or, perhaps both, and perhaps many times. I also realized that health problems are not so different from other crises many of us face; separation and/or divorce, bankruptcy, flood or fire, legal problems, job loss or job insecurity, family conflict, etc., etc.

How do we move with grace and equanimity through all the many challenges life presents to us?

The greatest obstacle to choosing happiness is our tendency to dwell in either the past or the future. We fixate on the past in order to try to predict the future to give ourselves the illusion of control. We then project what happened in the past onto the future and paint all kind of horrible scenarios that can literally drive us nuts.

But what happened in the past, is not necessarily

a predictor of the future (unless it is clothed in expectation).

Choosing happiness means accepting responsibility for what you can control and acting on it. But it also means letting go of the past, as well as speculation about the future when there is nothing else you can do.

Expect that everything will be OK, and if it's not OK, then believe in yourself enough to know that you will have the strength and wisdom to deal with it at the time.

Opt to live in the present, to offer love, compassion and humor when the time is right. Only then can you appreciate the blessings that each moment brings, and allow them to bring happiness if only for a brief sweet interlude between the tears.

The second greatest obstacle to choosing happiness is the mostly unconscious, and incredibly ancient belief that hardship, crises, ill health and problems of all stripes are some kind of divine punishment meted out to those that are evil, unworthy, incompetent or lazy. Even if our minds tell us this is balderdash, our emotions are still tuned to the energy of this cultural legacy.

When we have problems we often feel judged by others, and if not by them, by ourselves. As long as we feel like we are not measuring up, that our problems are the result of some bad deed, or being an inferior or "bad" person, it is hard to choose happiness because down deep inside, we don't believe we deserve it.

Becoming aware of this cultural myth (and our responses to it when something goes wrong), is the first step in releasing it.

Taking on this collective guilt is bad enough, but rejecting it without further thought may be even worse.

If you know you do not qualify as unworthy or culpable, yet still believe the myth of reward and punishment, then you must be a victim. "I don't deserve this." As long as your condition is the fault of somebody else (or the system or the situation or whatever), then you have no responsibility for it, and as such, no ability to change it. Then you become a victim.

Victims are by definition unhappy people.

The more challenges we face in life, the more capable and competent we are. The more problems we tackle, the more possibilities to gain wisdom and compassion. The more difficult the problem, the more creative we become.

The universe is not out to punish anyone. It is designed to steer us toward our highest potential.

We can choose to be happy even in the midst of the messiness of life if we understand that our value to the universe increases exponentially with every problem we face. The Earth is not an easy assignment, but since we all volunteered, we are honored and respected for our courage and commitment, for our wisdom and creativity, and for our ability to love.

Know you are loved and valued even as you struggle. Then choose to be happy, to practice love, tenderness and humor even if the midst of chaos, (and don't forget the chocolate!)

14
Floating Potentials

When we understand how expectation and synchronicity work, we can begin to practice simple manifestation.

Manifestation happens when we float potentials out into the universe that we would like to bring to reality. They can be the solutions to very large complex problems like intra-family harmony or a new sustainable energy source, or they can be simple everyday needs. In order to hone your manifesting skills however, it's best to start with the small stuff.

Floating potentials also means not limiting yourself to what you know (or think) is possible, especially as you tackle bigger and more complex issues.

Assuming we know what is possible and what is not possible automatically confines us to a very small box.

Thinking "outside the box" is a very popular term these days. Everyone wants innovation and ingenuity, but how do we do it? What really goes into thinking "outside the box", or better yet, how do we get beyond the "box" of the possible?

A conversation with a friend prompted me to think about this subject. She was complaining about her boss, who everyone in her department considers a very poor manager. Many of her colleagues are even thinking about leaving the company because of this person's poor management style.

But this person is pregnant, and scheduled for maternity leave in a few months. I suggested to my friend that perhaps her boss would love parenting so much that she would stay home with her baby. "Oh no," my friend replied. "She is wedded to her job. She would never even consider being a stay-at-home mom". And this opinion was apparently shared by everyone else in the department.

My friend has never been a mom, but I have. I never considered being a stay-at-home mom either. When my first baby was born, I changed my tune, so I know it's not impossible.

But it does seem impossible for my friend and all her colleagues, none of whom are moms either. As long as my friend and her colleagues (and her boss) think it's impossible, it IS impossible. For them, the option of staying home really doesn't exist.

Thinking outside the box means allowing yourself to contemplate as possible, things that you thought previously were impossible. The "box" is simply what you believe is possible, and a "box" is a wonderful metaphor.

What we think is possible is terribly confining.

We use our hands to create entirely new items out of physical matter. Likewise, our consciousness organizes energy to create new potentials.

When you allow yourself to believe something is possible that you didn't believe was possible before, you introduce a new potential, that is, an organized energy field that didn't exist previously. Once a potential is introduced, it is able to gather the additional energy it needs to become actualized.

In my friend's case, choosing to be a stay-at-home mom is not a new potential, but it is a new potential for my friend and her colleagues. If one of them "floats" this potential, that is, begins to think of it as a real possibility for her boss, and also begins to activate it by giving it energy (attention), it becomes more available as a potential for others as well. Once it is "floated", others can connect with it and give it their energy (begin to believe it's possible), thus activating it further and increasing the chances that the boss will connect to it as well, and honestly consider it for herself.

I use the word "floating" because this all happens on the energetic level, and this is the beauty of it. There is no agenda, no coercion, no necessity for the boss to feel defensive, because it is an idea that is simply "floating", that is, available for all to connect with if they choose.

Floating potentials for others does not necessarily mean that the potential will actualize in reality. If my friend "floats" this potential in her workplace, it does not mean her boss will actually choose to stay home. But it certainly does increase the probability that this could happen.

This kind of manifestation is a way of offering possibilities to others that they may not have thought about themselves. It is also a way of putting out into the universe original ideas that you may not have the ability to actualize yourself. When you float these kind of ideas, they then become available for those better equipped to bring them to fruition.

The fact that there is no force involved leaves others free to choose something that appears to be their own idea. They are also free not to choose. Ultimately, we have no control, nor should we have control, over what another person chooses for themselves.

When you float potentials for yourself, however, the outcome can be far more magical and amazing.

You do have a choice over what you believe is possible, and whether to change that belief. You also have a choice as to what potentials you choose, and how much energy and attention you give them.

If you dare to think beyond what you would ordinarily believe is possible, and become passionate about achieving this goal for yourself, you draw an enormous amount of energy to your project or goal. This influx of energy often inspires others, and they also provide energy. Before long, what was once impossible, graduates from potential, to actual reality.

It's pretty amazing what we humans can accomplish once we get beyond our "boxes".

As we begin to think beyond the box of the possible, it is important to start small, with simple needs that are not really that important. This takes the stress out of the process since it doesn't really matter if your experiment works.

Here are some examples from my own life after I decided to start practicing simple manifestation.

Years ago, after I first learned about manifestation, I was walking my dogs on our country road and noticed a lot of litter on the roadside. I tried to gather some of it, but gave up quickly because there was so much and I had nowhere to put it..

Then I wondered if perhaps I could manifest a bag? So I imagined a white plastic bag with handles lying on the side of the road, and floated that idea gently out into the universe to gather energy. Then I forgot about it and continued my walk.

At the end of the road where I usually turn around, there, on the side of the road, was a white plastic bag with handles, exactly as I had imagined. I picked it up and marveled at its presence. I was delighted with this seemingly magical materialization.

With this bag, I was able to gather all the litter on the roadside on my return home. The bag was just the right size with not an inch to spare.

On another occasion, I was cleaning the spare room for weekend guests, when I decided I needed a small bedside table for a lamp. I imagined just the kind of table I wanted, and floated that potential.

I knew the table I had in mind could only be found at an antique store, so I got in the car and went directly to the only antique store in our small town. And there, on the second floor right in front of the stairs, was the exact table I had imagined, at a price I could afford.

Trust that the potentials you float will manifest if they are in your best interest and in the best interest of the rest of the universe. Then you don't have to worry about messing up anybody or anything.

If they don't manifest, then there is something else going on that you are not aware of, and the fact that they didn't manifest is probably for the best.

It could mean that there is a lack of coherence between you and your intention. It could mean that there would be unintended negative consequences, or that there is something better out there that you haven't yet thought of.

Manifestation is a co-creative process between you and your soul and the energy at its command. Trust yourself and the process, and then experience the magic.

15
Change vs. Transformation

Change in the physical world is hard.

This is because matter is a very dense energy vibrating very slowly, and its natural state is one of stasis or rest. Moving physical matter from this natural state of rest takes much work, effort, and also some kind of force. Since the physical world is the only reality we have known until now, change through work, effort and force is the only way we know how to change anything, including ourselves.

Today we are beginning to recognize that we are not only physical beings, but energy beings as well. In fact, our energetic bodies are much larger and more powerful than our physical bodies.

Our efforts to change in the past have often failed

largely because we were trying to use the rules of the physical world to change ourselves, that is, to change something that is mostly energy. In order to change energy, we have to use energetic rules, not physical ones. Our efforts to change ourselves are therefore not terribly successful most of the time.

In the world of energy, change is much easier than in the physical realm, which is why I choose to call it "transformation" rather than "change". The natural state of energy is flow or movement rather than stasis. It is much easier to change something that is moving than something that is at rest.

Imagine the difference between moving a large flat rock and guiding a moving bicycle. Moving a large flat rock takes much effort and force, while guiding a moving bicycle takes only a slight wrist movement. In fact, too much effort, too much force on the handlebars of the bicycle would result in complete disaster.

Think also about the rules of martial arts (which are based on rules of energy), where the student is taught not to resist his opponent but rather to join with the force or motion the opponent is already using, and redirect it another way.

When we try to force ourselves to change, we encounter a natural internal resistance that comes from using physical rules in the wrong dimension. The secret is to find the energy behind the habit or behavior we want to change and then redirect it in a more constructive way.

If overeating is a behavior you would like to transform, think about why you overeat. I tend to overeat because I really like food. I love the taste, the texture and the combination of flavors found in really good food. Therefore, the thought of dieting brings immediate resistance, because I am restricting the flow of energy to something I enjoy.

Using my knowledge of energy, my solution to overeating is to eat much more slowly, chew well, savoring each bite as long as possible, and to drink water in between bites to clear my palate for the next bite.

I also decided to restrict my food intake only to foods I really love (why eat anything else?). Before I put anything in my mouth, I now ask myself if this is something I really would enjoy? If the answer is no, then I it is much easier to decline. Consequently, I no longer overeat and I enjoy my food much more. It's a win-win all around.

If worry is your principle stressor and you would like to change this tendency, think about the energy behind the worry, in other words, what benefits it brings you. We usually worry because we know bad things can happen and we want to avoid them as much as possible. We know that if we think about what bad things can happen and take precautions to avoid them, we are often successful.

The problem is, there are only some things that we have control over, and many others we can do nothing about. Worrying about those things is pointless and brings no benefit, only stress.

When you find yourself worrying, ask yourself if this is something you can do something about.

If it is, do it. Expect the best but prepare for the worst. Then let it go.

If it is something that you can do nothing about, you can choose to trust that things will work out.

Worrying is just using your imagination to bring you things you don't want (remember, similarities attract).

Trusting, on the other hand, is using your imagination to bring you what you do want, because attention, intention and imagination are what move and direct energy.

Learning to trust is not easy because we are habituated to the physical world where change happens only as a result of cause and effect with work, effort and force as the cause. In order to avoid unpleasant experiences in the past, we have learned to expect that a certain cause will always bring the same result as in the past.

Negative expectations based on the past are therefore one of the greatest barriers in learning to trust. Not trusting is one of the greatest factors in blocking transformation.

Trusting allows you to "enter the flow" of universal energy, so that, just like a river, it carries us effortlessly along with it. Energy is constantly in motion. When we "enter the flow", we seek to harmonize our energy with the flow of the universe so that moving is easy, and change, (in this case, transformation) is just a part of the process.

Section Four

Understanding Duality

16

On the Necessity of Duality

One other great barrier to trust is the emphasis on duality that dominates the physical world.

The duality inherent in physical life seems to be especially intense these days. We see it in partisan politics, in civil wars around the world, in social inequality and even in our own personal lives where we find ourselves criticizing and feeling estranged from those we thought were "like us".

Although duality often takes the form of conflict and strife, it is essential in physical life because it helps us distinguish what is "good", or life giving (an apple) and what is "bad" or life threatening (a rattlesnake). Our emotions are programmed to respond this way, and our ego translates emotional information into clear dictates about what is good for us and bad for us.

Without being able to make these distinctions we would not remain long on Earth.

Unfortunately, what is physically good and bad for us, is easily transferred into our psychological life. Good and bad then become judgments about other people and other things that often have nothing to do with our actual well-being, but rather reflect our belief systems and our need to validate ourselves by being surrounded by others who are similar.

Therefore, we tend to put situations and people into absolute categories labeled "good" and "bad".

In other words, what started as an instinctual survival mechanism can easily become subverted by the ego's need to validate its own self-worth. As long as we look for validation outside of ourselves, this will always be a problem.

Duality is also important for the growth of consciousness. It is only through absolute opposition that we are able to bring new things into our awareness.

A small child raised in a house with a small short-haired pet, soon learns this animal is called a dog. One day he and his mother visit a neighbor's house where there is a cat. The child points at the cat and says, "dog".

What is the first thing the mother says to him?

Most likely she will not say, "That is a cat". First, she must say, "That is NOT a dog".

Absolute opposition, that is, "dog vs NOT dog", is first necessary for the child to discover a new concept. First, he must understand that what he thinks he is seeing is not what he thought. Only then can he begin to process the new information.

Ironically, the growth of consciousness is not only a product of duality, it is also the way to move beyond duality and understand its true nature.

A small child must first process the difference between dogs and cats as an absolute opposite in order to integrate a new concept. Once that concept is internalized however, the child is then free to conceptualize the oppositions, that is, to realize that this opposition is only a relative opposition or concept, not an absolute.

Before long he realizes that dogs and cats are both mammals, and are really more alike than different given all the other animals on Earth.

When we conceptualize opposition, we realize we can use this ability to organize and categorize in order to find either opposition or similarity in just about anything. Through this mental process, we can begin to use conceptualization to take the emotional impact of duality out of our personal lives.

As we reflect on our ability to conceptualize, we

realize we can use conscious awareness to seek similarities where before we only saw only differences.

Consciousness awareness can help us realize that a friend's path to spiritual growth may be different from ours, but we are both seeking the same thing. It helps us understand that black people and white people are both just people, with the same desire to grow and evolve and be respected and valued by others.

Awareness cuts through the fog, bringing the realization that despite the nasty rhetoric, politicians on both sides of the aisle have more in common with each other than with most of their constituents.

When we focus conscious awareness on duality, we understand opposition as a functional tool.

We then no longer need to be victims of our emotional reactions, even though we may still have them. Awareness allows us to see opposition and similarity at the same time. It gives us the full picture rather than a partial image. It takes us above and outside of ourselves.

In this way, our awareness expands to the soul level, where compassion and blessings for all creation fill our hearts and open our minds with insight and wisdom.

17

Darkness and Light

In learning to conceptualize duality, it is useful to use darkness and light as metaphors for duality in general.

Darkness and light both exist, and are both necessary, but are meant to be in balance. Balance between them ensures that we see each clearly for what it is. When darkness and light are balanced, the presence of darkness helps us choose light.

Darkness is only a problem when it is hidden.

When darkness is hidden, it sees only itself.

When darkness is hidden, it can multiply, grow and pervert its environment.

When darkness is hidden, it can operate freely without hindrance.

Then balance is lost.

Today, the world seems full of darkness: ISIS, homegrown terrorists, school shooters, corruption in government, coercion and manipulation in business, race, gender and sexual orientation bias, and inequality in economic distribution and in racial and ethnic justice, to name a few.

At this time, the human condition seems dire, with cruelty and injustice assaulting our senses from all directions. It is easy to lapse into depression and despair.

But what is being revealed to us now is not new. It has always been there despite romantic and/or idealistic memories of the "good old days". The old days were "good" only because so much was hidden.

Darkness was hidden behind a consciousness that didn't see it, that had not evolved to a point where it could recognize the many kinds of darkness.

In the "good old days" it was OK to beat a wife or child, have sex with a woman against her will, slaughter noncombatants in war (collateral damage), torture people to try to get information, and deceive people (lie) in order to make a sale or get elected. It was noble to kill in the name of a religion or ethnic group, pick off assumed enemies with sniper fire, or force a hostile takeover only to bankrupt the company for personal gain.

Darkness was hidden because systems of communication were limited (no internet of cell phone cameras), and both reporters and the justice system had a code of silence when it came to important people or privileged groups using drugs, having affairs, inappropriate sexual relationships, or shady, illegal, or corrupt business and/or political dealings.

It was hidden because countries that oppressed women and massacred minorities seemed far away and out of sight. We did not know about female genital mutilation or child brides. We were only vaguely aware of mass genocides taking place in Africa and other third world countries.

Darkness was hidden because people who were different changed their names, hid in closets, lived a lie and closely guarded their secrets. Rape was thought to be the fault of the woman and thus a thing of shame never to be spoken of by the victim herself.

Are there more rapes today than in the past?

Probably not, it's just that society, and particularly young men are finally seeing rape as a crime, and consequently women are speaking out against their attackers much more frequently.

Is there more abuse of power than there used to be?

In fact, there is probably less, because we are finally waking up to the fact that power is a weapon that can be used to inflict great harm on both individuals and society. We are currently rearranging our feelings about power: who should have it, and appropriate and inappropriate uses of it.

Are there more wars today than ever before?

Despite the turmoil in the Middle East, the world is quite peaceful compared to the past. The website *Our World in Data* (www.ourworlddata.org/war-and-peace/) has a number of charts and graphs that are quite helpful in understanding the relative peace in which we now live.

The physical and mental wounding of our veterans along with the atrocities of terrorist groups flashing on our television or computer screens, are making war seem less and less an efficient, effective or civilized means of solving global problems.

Is there more crime today than in the past?

In fact, violent crime in most major cities has gone down quite dramatically in the past decade, even though there are constant small ups and downs that many in power use to try to make us afraid.

Today, at the beginning of the 21st century the world is changing rapidly, and in a good way, believe it or not. All the rocks are being turned over and the ugly creepy-crawlies hidden there are being exposed for all to see.

Although it seems awful to those of us who have to watch, these unsavory creatures now have nowhere to hide and will consume each other in their efforts to avoid responsibility for what they have done. While what is being revealed is extremely distasteful and depressing, what we are seeing is light and dark seeking to balance themselves.

"Lucifer" means "light bringer". It is only through darkness that we can truly recognize, and then choose, light.

18

The Nature of Evil

Lucifer is also one of the names that our culture has given the Devil, our personification of evil. But our Western cultural understanding of evil is at best inconsistent and at worst schizophrenic.

Many of us raised in the West have been taught that evil is a real entity who lurks outside us and can influence us or even take over our bodies, and even our souls.

On the other hand, we are also told that evil and sinfulness are inside us. Because we are born in sin we need an outside entity (like a savior) to release us from our evil nature.

The fact that evil exists certainly can't be denied. We see evidence of it all the time. But how can evil

It's All About Energy: Adventures in Expanded Reality

be both inside us and outside us at the same time? If God is love, why does evil exist in the first place?

Most people's reaction to evil is to get as far away from it as possible. We isolate ourselves in "safe" neighborhoods or gated communities. We lock up convicted felons and drug addicts, hoping to insulate and protect ourselves.

But we may actually be running in the wrong direction.

Many years ago, I was granted a profound lesson about the true identity of evil. After a long and close relationship with my first spirit guide, I asked him if he would show me an image of his face, (since I had always interacted with him strictly as an energy being before this point).

He agreed, and with my eyes closed, I began to see an image slowly begin to form in the lower left quadrant of my mind's eye.

The face that materialized was radiant with unconditional love, compassion and understanding. It was the most beautiful face I have ever seen, with features that were exquisite in their perfection. I was amazed and transfixed.

As I was gazing in wonder and delight at this incredible image, I began to notice movement in the upper right quadrant of my inner vision, as if some other face was trying to emerge. I didn't want to be distracted from the wondrous beauty before me, but much to my irritation, the second image continued to demand my attention, and I was at last forced to direct my focus there.

To my horror, the image I found was the exact opposite of the first face.

It was the most evil, disgusting, cruel visage I had ever encountered. It oozed malevolence and deceit with a mouth twisted in a mocking leer. I was at once repulsed and enraged, and demanded to know why my guide would show me this horrible face side-by-side with the other.

"This is also my face," he said. "And it is your face as well. There is no such thing as a good person or a bad person. Every human is a whole with the potential for both absolute good and absolute evil. What makes the difference is choice."

With his words also came the understanding that embracing our wholeness means accepting our capacity for evil as well as our capacity for good.

It is only with this understanding of our full potential that we have the ability to clearly exercise choice. Choice is conscious, and if I am unconscious of my capacity for evil, I cannot consciously choose between good and evil.

This means I am vulnerable to unconscious actions or words that happen reflexively without true choice. The greatest source of evil is the illusion that a "good" person could not possibly commit evil.

Most evil can be traced to three factors; fear, power and ignorance.

Even the most loving and loyal family dog will bite when frightened and cornered. If I do not appreciate my capacity for evil, I can easily be caught off guard when badly frightened, and pull the trigger reflexively only to find it was my best friend playing a joke.

If I understand my wholeness I will be more responsible with dangerous things and more aware of my ability to hurt or harm with words and deeds, even when frightened or threatened.

Most people first seek power to overcome vulnerability (another form of fear). Once power is experienced, however, it can easily become addictive.

A person may initially seek power to protect himself, but the rush that comes with power often seduces him/her to do whatever is needed to acquire more. Understanding power seeking behavior as an addiction can help us moderate our own need for power as well as help us find creative ways to help others become aware of the destructiveness that inevitably results from the abuse of power.

Most of all, evil is caused by ignorance.

How many times have we innocently said or done something which later caused irreparable harm. We long to take back our words or undo our actions, never having dreamed they could cause so much damage.

But good choices can only be built on a foundation of bad choices. It is only through our experience with evil that we gain the understanding and awareness to consciously choose.

Evil exists outside only through the fact that like energy attracts like energy. Those that choose evil through impulsive reaction, thirst for power, or ignorance will attract others who do the same. Evil exists inside us because it is part of our wholeness. We need no outside help to save us however, because divinity is also a part of that wholeness.

Embracing this wholeness empowers us to choose wisely.

It is also through the awareness of our own capacity for evil, that we are able to extend the light of unconditional love, forgiveness and compassion to those who perpetrate evil, whether because of fear, addiction or ignorance. It is much harder to judge and condemn when we can see both ourselves and others as whole.

Wholeness allows the light and the dark to dance together, and move us forward as a human species.

19
The Law of Reaction

What makes things darkest just before the dawn?

The Law of Reaction insures that extremes will never fly completely apart. Instead, when one extreme reaches its absolute pole, reaction will send the momentum back the other way. This law is similar to the Law of Karma except the Law of Reaction applies to cultures and large groups rather than individuals.

Because human beings are both energy beings and physical beings, they participate in both the duality of physical reality and the complementarity of opposites in the energy realm. In other words, humans will experience the extremes of experience throughout their many lives, but that experience is always balanced by an opposite but complementary experience.

If they experience one extreme at one point in their lives, they will necessarily also experience the opposite at another point. These two opposite extremes then complement each other by bringing wisdom and compassion.

Only through these experiences of absolute opposition can an individual come to a center point where he or she has experienced both and is thus able to make a clear choice about which is preferred. Clear choice is only possible when you have experience with what you are choosing.

If you are offered two different foods, one that you know and one that you don't know, you will probably choose the one you know, even if you don't like it much. You simply don't have the information you need to make an informed choice.

The Law of Karma is NOT punishment.

Instead, Karma allows human beings to experience polar extremes so they have the experience and the knowledge to make informed choices. Choices can't be informed if one choice is clouded in ignorance.

Karma is a spiritual necessity because it enables the evolution of both consciousness and compassionate understanding. It is much easier to feel compassion and understanding for those walking on paths we have also walked, because only then do we know what it is like. Only then can we choose with true wisdom and knowledge.

If I have been a drug addict either in this life or another, or I have a loved one who is a drug addict, I have the experience to make informed choices about the best way to help addicts.

If I have been an addict I know that being thrown in jail with other addicts and violent criminals makes the problem worse, not better. If I have been an addict, I do not seek punishment or retribution for the drug offender, but rather the best means of rehabilitation. If I have a loved one who is an addict, I can easily see that providing good therapy is far more cost effective and productive than prison time.

But if I have never been a drug addict myself, or known loved ones who have been addicted, I am afraid of their irrational behavior, and inclined to vilify them and see them as "other" and/or dangerous. It is easy to castigate them for their poor choices and want to punish them for making those choices.

It is this kind of thinking that justifies cruel and inhumane treatment, and makes us want to hide them away in prisons and jails.

It is only by having direct experience with addiction that our perceptions change. Only then can our choices about how to think and how to act be truly well informed.

Once we have experienced enough of life's polarities to develop compassion and understanding about life and our fellow humans, we no longer need to experience extremes, and can step out of the cycle of Karma.

The Law of Reaction is a corollary to the Law of Karma but acts on a national or cultural level. It allows cultures the experiences needed to make informed choices in the same way the Law of Karma works for individuals.

Homosexuality, for example, was long condemned by American culture. Gays and lesbians hid in their closets, afraid to expose themselves to ridicule, condemnation and violence, so no one knew how many there were, or that your family member or neighbor or even you, yourself might be Gay. People condemned LGBTQ people because they were different, and most people didn't think they knew anyone like that. People even condemned themselves when they thought they might fall into this category.

Then Gay men started to get AIDS.

As devastating as HIV/AIDS has been for the Gay community, I believe it also is a direct cause of the amazing changes in LGBTQ acceptance in the time since this disease was discovered.

Once Gay men started to get AIDS, they couldn't hide anymore. As a result, the Gay population seemed to grow. This was because those who had AIDS couldn't hide and their friends and lovers who didn't have AIDS felt they couldn't hide anymore either.

Although many people saw AIDS as God's judgment of Gay people, and violence against them grew, the suffering inflicted by both the disease and the subsequent anti-gay violence, created a backlash of support (a reaction). People recognized their LGBTQ family members and neighbors as the same people they had loved before. It was hard to abandon newly de-closeted friends and family just because they had a different sexual orientation.

Today there are still those who condemn homosexuality, but many more have now embraced their LGBTQ friends and family members, with a majority of the American people now supporting marriage equality. We have experienced both sides of the issue and now have the wisdom needed to make an informed choice.

For most of us, that informed choice is for compassion, acceptance and love.

The Law of Reaction leads us as a culture or nation through the extremes of one side in order to facilitate a reaction that moves us to the other side. Once we have experienced both polarities, we can make informed choices.

Homosexuality was hidden and therefore unexperienced by most of us. But now we have seen it in the light of day, and know we don't need to be afraid anymore. We now see LGBTQ people not as "other", but rather as human beings just like us who bring unique perspectives into our lives.

Once we have experienced both sides of an issue and can make informed choices, extreme swings are no longer needed. But even if our culture is still in need of polarities of experience, we, as individuals, need not be affected if we are already seeing the world with non-dual awareness.

We will, of course, still feel tremendous compassion for those affected by extremes, but through our own wisdom and trust we need not suffer ourselves even though our environment may seem chaotic and irrational.

As you see our culture descend into the depths of one extreme position after the other, remember the Law of Reaction.

Every action has a reaction. Every extreme will cause a counter movement. It is only through experiencing the extremes of both polarities that we, as a species, gain the wisdom to make informed choices. It is these informed choices that guide the evolution of humanity.

Section Five
Relationships With Others

20
Energy Stealing

When someone steals our physical possessions, or attacks or injures our physical body, we have recourse to the legal system.

As a society, we believe it is wrong to steal money or possessions, or injure another person physically. But energy is invisible and intangible, so most of us have not yet recognized that it's possible for people to take this vital ingredient from us. As a result, all of us steal energy, some to a greater extent than others.

Just like food, humans need energy to survive.

We've all heard about the babies in orphanages who were given good food and physical care, but died anyway because no one gave them the love and attention they needed. Attention is energy, and love is an even more potent form of energy.

Food feeds our physical bodies, but our energy bodies need to be fed as well, and we will languish and fade without this important nourishment.

Babies learn early how to get energy from their parents. They smile, laugh, act really cute, cry or have tantrums. For some children, good grades are a sure attention-getter, while for others athletic prowess wins the day. Whatever works. If positive energy, (unconditional love and caring), is not available, children will act out, for even negative attention is better than nothing.

As adults, when feeling depleted, we seek energy (attention) from those around us, just as we did as children.

Since energy is not visible and most people don't recognize it as a need, we have no cultural rules governing how we acquire energy when we need it. But just like there are legal and illegal ways to acquire material objects, there are both healthy and unhealthy ways to acquire energy. When faced with someone using illegitimate means, we may not know exactly what is happening to us, but we definitely feel that something is very wrong.

People steal energy when they take another's energy without permission and without equal exchange.

This is a doubly pernicious form of theft because it usually goes on outside the consciousness of both parties involved. In other words, people who steal energy usually are not aware that they are doing it, and people from whom they steal are usually not consciously aware of what is going on either. Only afterwards will they feel exhausted, drained, coerced, manipulated, or that something very unsavory has happened, even when they don't know exactly what.

There are many different levels of energy stealing, from the most subtle to the most obvious. Any attention seeking behavior is an attempt to acquire energy, whether it's dominating a business meeting, stonewalling a vote or a project, intimidating a co-worker, talking all the time, or being the class clown or drama queen.

One example of a very obvious form of energy stealing is the person with the vacuum eyes, that is, a person who drains energy from others just by being in the same room. This person doesn't even have to say anything to do the job. The sucking happens unconsciously and without any overt physical manifestation, but leaves its victims drained and confused, not understanding what happened.

Others suck energy verbally, by monopolizing the conversation, not pausing to let the other person talk, or always turning the conversation back to themselves.

When this kind of person talks constantly about their own problems (the victim), the energy sucking is even worse because of the implication that the energy sucker not only needs energy, but physical help as well.

People will often try to manipulate you into giving your permission for them to steal energy. They try to convince you that they have something you want in exchange for what they need, even though you are not particularly interested. At first their offer may seem quite reasonable, but you somehow know that if you refuse, they will steal your energy anyway. For example, they might offer their services for free, (and they may be very good at what they do). It is only later that you realize the price you are paying.

Coercion is energy stealing with no pretense. The person threatens you with some form of unwanted consequence if you fail to do what they want.

One of the most pernicious examples of this form of energy stealing is conditional love. I will love you but only if you do/are what I want you to do/be. This kind of person often feeds off of what you are or have, that is, they live vicariously through you. If you change or refuse to do or be what they need, it threatens them because you are removing an important source of nourishment.

Power seeking behavior is one of the worst forms of energy stealing. The more power a person has over you, the more energy they can steal, and the less you can do about it. Power seeking behavior comes in all forms, from cruel despotic kings and dictators to spiritual gurus.

In this most severe form of energy stealing, the thief can take not just your subtle energy, but your physical resources as well: your money, your job or even your life. Whenever someone makes you an offer you can't refuse, they are stealing your energy. This is why power is so addictive.

The power seeker will usually offer you something in return, protection, votes, favorable treatment, or even the promise of their attention. The more energy a person needs from others, the more vulnerable they are to the power seeker.

The reason most of us steal energy in some form or another is because we believe energy to be finite like all physical resources. After all, if there is only so much water, so much oil, so much land, so much money, then energy must be limited as well.

We seek energy from each other because we don't know where else to get it.

The good news is that energy is not finite and there are healthy ways to exchange energy with other people, as well as ways to create energy for ourselves without having to get it from others.

Healthy social energy exchange is when both people freely give of their energy to each other, not because they have to, but because they want to.

For example, two friends go to lunch and each has time to talk about themselves and their concerns while the other listens. Then they might talk about something of mutual interest. They laugh a lot and enjoy each other's company, and each comes away feeling refreshed and renewed. Each person knows they can count on the other to be there when perhaps they are going through hard times and need extra energy. But both know they will reciprocate and it will all come out even in the end.

Unlike the exchange of physical things, energetic exchange of this kind has a magical quality.

If I give you a loaf of bread and you give me a loaf of bread, neither of us wins or loses. When energy is freely and equitably exchanged by two people however, it multiplies exponentially. In other words, both people get far more energy out of the interaction than they put into it. It is win-win for both.

In addition, other humans are not the only resource when it comes to energy.

Unlike physical resources, energy is not finite. There is an infinite Source of energy available to us all the time, free for the taking.

One of the best ways to access this Source is through meditation. You can use the first guided imagery available at the end of this book to get started. After using the meditation for a while, just simple intention can bring energy in from Source any time you need it. Knowing this Source is always available can put burnout behind you, as well as help restore a passion for life.

Laughter and artistic creation are two other excellent ways to generate energy.

Laughter is healing and energizing. We need much more of it in our lives. Humor eases psychological conflict and helps us integrate uncomfortable truths.

Artistic creation is an expression of the soul. Whether it's singing, painting, gardening, making a rock wall, wood-working, writing in a journal or just doodling, any kind of creation can be energizing as long as we relax into it, and don't bash ourselves for not being "artistic".

And finally, the very best way to generate energy is to learn to love ourselves unconditionally (a tall order but well worth the effort). Loving ourselves means we don't need to depend on others for our sense of value. Self-love generates its own energy which means we need far less energy than people who have not yet developed this ability.

Unconditional love for self also brings the ability to love others unconditionally. When we need nothing from others, we are free to give generously and choose consciously where and with whom we share.

21

The Origin of Vampires

Ever since seeing the first Dracula movie with Bela Lugosi as a teenager, I have been fascinated with vampires.

In that movie, Dracula has such a strange combination of characteristics; bloodlust, cruelty, seductiveness, and even sensitivity, that he was oddly appealing. I both loved and hated him, but I had a hard time explaining these conflicting emotions to myself. It was just a story, and a pretty disgusting one at that.

Vampire myths and stories first became popularized in the early 18th century and have been found in many forms ever since. But you can hardly fail to notice that vampires have become a really big thing in the beginning of the 21st century. From Stephanie Meyer's *Twilight* series to TV shows like *True Blood*, there are vampire tales everywhere. We've had these stories for 300 years, so why the surge in popularity today?

Myths and stories capture our attention and become popular because they concretize an idea or situation that is so subtle it eludes conscious awareness. The story or myth takes these phenomena and gives them form and structure so that we can begin to understand what is really happening. We may never become fully conscious of why we are so fascinated, but the story seems to help us make sense of our lives on some level.

Vampire tales are metaphoric references to energy stealing. They give form and structure to something we have all experienced, but which is nonetheless frightening because it is below the threshold of consciousness and therefore unprotected by societal rules. We don't understand consciously what is happening, why it is happening or how to stop it, so it becomes quite unsettling.

These stories use the metaphoric image of the vampire to give that scary energy a form, and then explain through narrative what is happening, and how to protect ourselves from the danger.

The vampire (energy sucker) appears human, and in many cases, can be quite appealing, so anyone could be one. You never know when you've been exposed until it is too late.

Although excessive energy sucking can kill you, most often you can save yourself if you can just get away in time and replenish what has been taken. Therefore, once bitten, you become an energy sucker too, preying on those around you just like you were preyed upon before.

Traditionally, so the story goes, you can protect yourself from vampires by holding a cross in front of you (once you know who they are, of course), a recognition that calling on spiritual energy can protect one from becoming a vampire. There is real truth in this part of the story, since once you learn to access spiritual energy (Source) and manage your own energy supply, you need never be depleted again, no matter how many energy suckers are around you.

Although older versions of vampire stories paint vampires as cruel and scary villains, there has always been something seductive, and even sympathetic about them.

They lure their victims with manipulation and trickery, and then feed on them, but only because they have to suck blood (energy) to keep functioning. It is a lose-lose proposition for the poor vampire – either he feeds or dies, just like energy sucking is for most people. We need to kill him to protect ourselves, but we're also sympathetic to his dilemma, because it is our dilemma too.

Modern versions of vampire stories, however, are treating vampires more compassionately. Today's vampires are sensitive, intelligent creatures who often know they have a problem and try to set rules for themselves so they can live in human society without doing harm.

This change in treatment demonstrates our culture's growing subconscious recognition that energy sucking is a universal human problem, and we need to be gentler with ourselves as we become aware of this inherent need. At the same time as we are coming to grips with this reality, we are trying to set rules for ourselves about how to move forward.

I believe that vampire stories are popular today because we are beginning to be more conscious of our need for energy, as well as concerned about how we get it.

Modern versions of vampire stories help us come to grips with this dilemma and offer some hopeful thoughts on the subject. Not all vampires are evil, nor do they necessarily have to endanger those around them. It is solely dependent on individual intention and choice.

Just like these new vampire characters, we humans also have choices about how we get what we need.

22

Energetic Abuse

There has been much in the news lately about domestic abuse.

Although focusing attention on physical abuse is certainly important, there are other kinds of abuse that need attention as well, namely emotional and energetic abuse. The effects of emotional abuse are now generally acknowledged, but we have yet to define and understand energetic abuse.

Physical abuse is concrete and obvious. When someone emerges with a black eye, broken nose, and/or cuts and bruises, we can prove that physical abuse has occurred. Someone who is physically stronger has inflicted injuries on someone who is weaker or who couldn't or wouldn't protect themselves.

Western culture now recognizes that physical abuse is wrong, even in the case of one's spouse or children, and we have laws to protect people from it.

We are also beginning to understand that emotional abuse can be just as damaging as physical abuse, if not more so. Calling someone a whore, a pervert, stupid, incompetent, or threatening them with bodily harm, can have long lasting psychological consequences, especially in children. We in the United States, however, have not yet decided how to treat emotional abuse legally, since free speech is protected by the constitution.

Energetic abuse is even more subtle, and occurs far more than we realize. Because it happens all the time, and because energy exchange is the underlying dynamic in all forms of abuse, it is vitally important that we learn to recognize and understand this kind of abuse.

Everyday energy stealing simply takes energy by commanding someone else's attention without giving an equal amount of energy back. Abusive energy stealing aims to steal far more. It wants not just energy, but the the most basic energy essence we have, our self-respect, self-confidence and sense of self, in short, our core identity.

The purpose of all abuse is to make people feel guilty, unworthy and/or powerless, thus shaking loose their self-esteem, self-respect and self-confidence.

Once this vital self-defining energy is called into question, the abuser can seize and claim it for his/her own. Consequently, physical, emotional and energetic abuse are all forms of energy stealing.

Unlike other forms of energy stealing however, abuse is characterized by an overt aggressive act that first throws the victim off balance and loosens personal energy so that it is easier to grab. Think of a purse snatcher bumping a victim in order to loosen her grasp and make the purse easier to take.

In physical abuse, this aggressive act is bodily harm. In emotional abuse it is name calling, swearing, taunting, threatening dire consequences or insulting or disrespectful behavior towards the victim. These aggressive acts are designed to pry away a person's self-respect and sense of worth by generating negative feelings of guilt, shame and/or self-loathing.

This loosened core energy is then appropriated by the abuser, giving him or her additional confidence and power.

The added energy and the abuser's ability to acquire it whenever needed, can lead to an almost addictive high, which then causes increasing use of these tactics to overcome feelings of inadequacy, fear, depression or powerlessness whenever they arise.

Energetic abuse is done for the same reasons, but because we cannot pinpoint a word or deed as the cause of our feelings of abuse, we are often surprised and confused by our feelings, further knocking us off balance. We feel like we've been punched in the gut, but can't really locate the cause even though we can usually identify the abuser. We know this person did something to unsettle and take something from us, but we can't figure out what happened or what exactly is missing.

Because energetic abuse happens on the subtle energy level, it can be much more effective than physical or emotional abuse because it is so deceptive and covert. It can happen through obstructional behaviors (such as procrastination, deceit, tardiness), subtle innuendo, underhanded or backhanded comments or behavior, or by ignoring someone completely.

Some common examples of energetic abuse are passive aggressive behavior and gaslighting.

Passive aggressive behavior is characterized by an unwillingness to be honest about negative feelings.

Instead, those negative feelings are expressed by resentful behavior like procrastination, avoidance and denial, as well as by energetic bombardment with hostile energy. A passive aggressive person will deny being angry even though being around him/her feels like dancing with a porcupine.

The lack of consistency between what the person is saying vs what s/he is doing and the kind of energy being put out results in confusion and uncertainty in victims that guarantees their continued attention (energy). The longer the negative feelings are verbally denied, the longer the passive aggressive person can commandeer the energy of those around him/her.

Even though the person denies being angry, his/her behavior broadcasts the unmistakable impression that the victim has done something terrible to the abuser and thus should feel guilty and ashamed.

Gas lighting is a tactic designed to undermine a person's perception of reality.

The gaslighter typically manipulates the situation so that the victim is continuously thrown off balance by inconsistencies between the abuser's definition of reality and the victim's perception of of what's really going on. In this way the victim's self-confidence, self-worth and ability to make decisions is eroded and depleted, thus opening the opportunity for the abuser to appropriate this energy for him/herself.

Energetic abuse also happens when someone dumps a great amount of negative energy on another person, usually while they are at the same time engaged in an innocuous conversation or activity. The disconnect between the energy dump and the overt speech or behavior is so great that we often feel like we are going insane or are in some alternate reality.

Another form of energetic abuse can occur when someone physically or energetically invades our energetic space. Sometimes it is done to directly appropriate energy, and other times for purposes of coercion and intimidation. Anything that is designed (either consciously or unconsciously) to undermine our free will is energy abuse.

Economic inequality is also a kind of energetic abuse.

Money is a symbol of energy. Even though corporate welfare and tax breaks for the wealthy cost governments far more than safety nets for people in need, the economically disadvantaged are made to feel guilty and unworthy for having to ask for help, or for struggling to make ends meet. Their condition is implied as a fitting punishment for their unworthiness, and helping them is often seen as condoning their "lazy" and "inept" lifestyle.

In this way, the wealthy and powerful (and wealthy powerful wannabes) take far more from people in poverty than just money. They are also taking self-respect, self-confidence and self-empowerment, and then adding this energy to the enormous amount they already have.

The exercise of power is one of the most pernicious kinds of energetic abuse.

A powerful person is in a position to steal energy anytime, anywhere, and in a variety of different ways. A person with power can command people's attention at all times for many reasons.

The first of these is fear.

Most people fear the person with power, and rightly so, because powerful people can control others' lives. And fear is the ultimate attention getter. If you are afraid of someone, you pay strict attention to everything they do or say, hoping your vigilance may somehow save you.

People in power steal energy by arbitrarily exerting control over other people, or by outright acts of coercion, physical, emotional or energetic abuse, and by disrespect. Even the act of ignoring someone steals energy. Any time one person can make another feel bad about themselves, that person is engaging in energetic abuse.

Some people might want to ask the person in power for favors, and there is no one who will gladly give more attention than a toady. The toady often realizes the price he/she is paying for the favor, and does it gladly, but may, in fact, be bled dry because of it. Then the toady will need to steal energy from someone else.

And some people just like to bask in the shadow of power, hoping it will rub off on them. They gladly give up their energy to the person in power, but then use that shadow of power to steal from others lower down on the ladder.

All these people are addicted to power.

Why do the wealthy and/or powerful need so much?

In most cases their needs are never satisfied because energy acquired from stealing can always be stolen away again. Energy gained this way is never secure. Under these conditions, they can never have too much because their hold on it seems so fragile.

Energy stealing can become addictive, and abuse is the most addictive form of energy stealing.

When a victim is thrown off balance by an aggressive act, whether physical, emotional or energetic, the amount and kind of energy available for capture is much greater in quantity and quality than in non-aggressive energy stealing.

This unusually large, intense intake of energy supplies a much greater jolt than normal energy stealing, and produces feelings of euphoria and self-importance in the abuser. It can be very difficult for someone to voluntarily get off this horse once s/he has gotten on.

It also should be noted that in almost all kinds of abuse, the perpetrator rarely commits the abuse consciously. Emotional feelings rise up and dictate certain actions geared to alleviate the emotional stress.

Even in physical abuse, where the consequences are obvious, many abusers are amazed that they caused injury, and sometimes remain in total denial, blaming the victim for causing the reaction. But once the high has been experienced, abusive tactics may be used automatically in order to alleviate any negative emotion.

The first step in preventing any kind of abuse is recognizing the various kinds of abuse and the many ways they are carried out.

23

Protecting Yourself

Once we understand the dynamics of abuse, we know not to allow ourselves to be thrown off balance by abusive behavior, whether it is physical, emotional or energetic. Efforts designed to belittle, coerce, threaten, make us feel guilty, unworthy or inconsequential are just ploys to loosen our self-confidence and make us vulnerable to giving up what is rightfully ours.

Basic energy management teaches us how to contract our energy fields in order to prevent energetic abuse.

In martial arts, the first lesson is learning how to bring your energy back to you and center it in your body. Centered energy increases strength and stability, decreasing the chance of being knocked off balance.

This lesson is important for protecting yourself emotionally and energetically as well as physically. When encountering a potentially abusive situation, remember to breathe deeply and draw your energy back to you. Center it in your Hara, just below the navel, and if you still feel vulnerable, ground your energy for added protection and strength. Once the energy field is centered and grounded, others can no longer steal, manipulate or otherwise become entangled in it.

Think of the ground (Earth) as an energy bank. Just like you put your hard-earned cash into the bank to keep it secure, the Earth provides a safe space to place your energy when you want to protect it from those wanting to steal or manipulate it. Unlike traditional banks, however, the Earth will calm, harmonize and smooth out your energy, as well as provide an unlimited supply to draw upon whenever you need it.

People who know how to tap the Earth and/or the Source for their energy needs, and/or generate energy through self-love, laughter, play and healthy social exchange, are truly empowered. They can freely share their energy with others because they have no fear that it can be taken away, or that they will be unable to generate more when needed.

There is no need to coerce, manipulate, deceive, threaten or abuse anyone. There is no need to control or dominate. They are sovereign beings, powerful in their own right with an inner strength and light that no one can take away. They use no force and have no agenda for others, because they know the only person they can really control, is themselves.

Abuse of all kinds says far more about the abuser than about the abused. By engaging in abusive behavior, the abuser is advertising his/her own deep emotional and energetic insecurity.

Do not allow the abuser to shake your confidence and sense of self. Instead regard the abuser with compassion and understanding while at the same time centering, and taking whatever measures necessary to avoid injury to yourself and any others that might also be at risk, even if it involves legal proceedings.

It is very difficult to change abusive behavior, so ultimately it is best to remove yourself from these kinds of people.

Unfortunately, sometimes we don't have that option. We all have co-workers, acquaintances, old friends, and/or immediate or extended family members with whom we must interact if not daily, at least from time to time.

Here are four things to remember when confronted with abusive and/or negative people.

1. Do not allow yourself to be drawn into the game.

Negative energy is emotional energy that is designed to create more negative energy. Remember, like energy attracts like energy.

When encountering negative energy, your first

response will also be negative. This is exactly what a negative person wants. Misery loves company, and complaining together is twice the fun. Abusive people also depend on people responding with fear or deference. Observe your response, then let it go, so that the more objective side of yourself can show up.

Negative and/or abusive people are very good at ferreting out your emotional buttons and knowing how to push them.

The more negative your reaction, the more buttons are being pushed. Learn to recognize your buttons and explore where they might have come from in your past. Once you gain this awareness it will be much easier to remain objective, and engage your energetic skills.

2. Stay focused on the positive.

Problems are presented to us so that we are challenged to find solutions, thus expanding our creativity and life experiences. Keep bringing the conversation back to solutions, but do not let others get away with making you responsible for solutions to their problems.

Abusive and/or negative people are good at seducing or coercing you into giving your energy away by accepting blame or responsibility for something that is not yours. This intention may be explicitly stated in words, but most often is just hovering around sucking you in without any words being spoken. It is especially prevalent in people who are unhappy with themselves and the world around them. These people find it easier to blame others rather than do the personal work necessary to make their lives better.

If people don't want to focus on solutions, change the subject to a more positive or neutral topic.

3. Learn to love and respect yourself.

Most of our emotional entanglements happen because we rely on the opinion of others and/or compare ourselves to others in order to gauge our own value.

If someone else criticizes us, compares us unfavorably or implies blame, we quickly allow this assessment to deflate our sense of self-worth and erode our self-confidence. Bullies are particularly good at undermining our self-confidence in order to steal energy.

Beware, beware, beware! This is a trap. Do not fall into it.

Criticism and comparison are the two most effective ways others steal our energy and our power. When another person makes you feel bad about yourself they are stealing your self-esteem in order to add it to their own.

If you allow them to make you feel bad, you are handing over your energy on a silver platter. This brand of energy of stealing is addictive. It's what makes bullies so vicious and relentless. The more they steal the better they feel, but they also know it's ephemeral power that can be stolen away again at any time, which is why they must steal more and more.

When you truly love and respect yourself, no one can steal your value or power because you know how to provide it for yourself. You don't need to rely on anyone else to supply it for you.

4. Cultivate a sense of humor.

Our sense of humor is one of the most beautiful gifts we humans have given ourselves. Psychologically, humor acts as a bridge between opposing ideas or situations. We often make jokes about things we are uncomfortable with because humor eases conflict.

Negative energy is a personal vibration that is chaotic, conflicted, incoherent, out-of-harmony and/or full of friction. Humor reduces the friction and adds positive energy to smooth things out. Laughter creates new energy when we are depleted, and reduces tension and stress. The ability to laugh at ourselves, and the situations in which we find ourselves, is especially healing.

These four tips are also invaluable in dealing with one's own negative cycles. All of us have our ups and downs. But when you get tired of pulling yourself under, treat yourself with loving kindness, and remember, it's just a game you can choose not to play.

Abuse is wrong, on any level.

24

Empathy and Anxiety

Empathy is a two-edged sword – it has its blessings and its curses.

Some people are empathetic because they have had many different experiences in life and can easily relate when others are going through the same thing. For these people, empathy is truly a blessing. It comes from a compassionate heart, and promotes loving connection.

Other people are empathetic because they are extremely energy sensitive and can sense other people's feelings as if they are their own. For these highly sensitive people, empathy can be a curse, (although it doesn't have to be).

If you are reading this book, there is a good chance you are already quite energy sensitive.

Even if you are not, as you increase your energy awareness, you may develop the kind of energy sensitivity described here. This chapter will give you tools to manage this gift, because energy sensitivity is truly a gift.

An energy sensitive person is much more easily affected by other people's moods, attitudes and problems. When those around us are happy and excited by life, there are no issues.

But when other people are throwing out negative emotions such as fear, anxiety, anger and frustration, those of us who are energy sensitive can be greatly affected. Without knowledge of energy, the rules that govern it, and how to manage our own energy fields, this sensitivity can be frightening because it seems as if something is the matter with us. We don't realize these feelings are almost always coming from outside ourselves.

How many times have you felt your mood change abruptly when walking into a room full of strangers; a doctor's waiting room, a college library or an airport waiting area, for example. All of a sudden you experience intense anxiety, or feel that everybody dislikes you for some reason, or that there is something wrong with your physical appearance or you get a headache or your heart starts pounding.

This abrupt change panics you further. What's wrong with me? Why is this happening? Do I need medical or psychological help?

Your immediate reaction is that there is something pathological going on.

But there is nothing wrong with you. You are simply picking up energy from those around you.

A doctor's waiting room is filled with people who are sick and in pain and anxious about what the doctor might tell them.

A college library is full of students nervous about upcoming tests or exams, or perhaps upset by romantic problems.

An airport gate area consists of hundreds of people dreading the tight uncomfortable flight experience and apprehensive about the possibility of delays, cancellations, baggage loss or even a crash. (Airports are also filled with people excited and happy about traveling, so if you experience negative energy in one spot, move to another and see if it feels better.)

Even group settings where other people's energy is more positive can be problematic. This is because the natural state of energy is coherence, which means that energy automatically wants to move toward entrainment and/or harmony.

When two tuning forks are struck together, they will start off singing different notes. After a few seconds, however, they will entrain themselves and begin to sound the same tone. Energy travels in waves just like sound, so an energy sensitive person will be most comfortable in situations where group energy is coherent and entrained.

Examples of these kind of group circumstances would be a class or workshop where everyone's attention is focused on the speaker. Concerts, plays and restaurants are also examples of venues where group energy is focused (on the entertainment, or on the food and the process of enjoying it).

A group situation like a party where there are numerous small groups talking amongst themselves, is an example of a less comfortable environment for an energy sensitive person. The party goers may all be having a good time, but because there are many small groups focused on many different conversations, the energy is not in sync and can often feel like fingernails scraping on a blackboard.

People in your immediate environment are not the only source of discomfort. At this time in our human evolution, the Earth is undergoing drastic changes because human consciousness is ready to move beyond ideas of limited resources, and us vs them belief patterns. In order for this to happen, however, many old systems must disintegrate so that new ones can be created.

These times are therefore quite chaotic, and we humans find chaos terribly anxiety provoking. Consequently, there is now mass anxiety on a global level, and the energy sensitive person can easily pick up on that as well.

Recently, I was out doing errands and had just parked in a large parking lot. All of a sudden I was overcome by an intense anxiety attack.

I quickly scanned my thoughts for anything that might have made me upset, and could find nothing.

I was alone out in the open with no humans close by who could be affecting me. I therefore concluded that this was simply an energetic response to something outside myself, so I pulled my energy back to me and let the anxiety go. In a few seconds, I was fine.

When anxiety or panic attacks happen out of the blue, first check your own thought processes to see if any conscious or subconscious thoughts have triggered this response. If not, then you've picked up energy from your environment because your energy field is open and available.

It can help to try to identify the source, but that isn't absolutely necessary to stop the attack. Just pull your energy back to you with your in-breath, and then ground it on the out-breath.

Allow the Earth to harmonize and entrain the frazzled energy you send her way, then pull whatever energy you need back to you and center it in your heart.

Heart centered energy allows you to be compassionate and empathetic to those around you without taking on their energy.

Use the first guided imagery in the appendix to hone your technique.

25

The Energy of Grievance

One of the ways the laws of energy differ from the laws of the physical world is that equal energy exchange is not a zero-sum game. In the physical world, the equal exchange of the same item leaves both people in the same situation as before. If I give you a glass of milk and you give me a glass of milk, we both end up with exactly what we started with.

In the energy world, however, equal exchange of energy results in that same energy multiplying exponentially.

When two friends go to lunch and both listen with attention and focus while each shares their news, thoughts and concerns, both people leave the encounter feeling energized and inspired, having received far more energy than they gave out.

When two or more collaborators exchange ideas openly and with no thoughts of competition, criticism or distrust, those ideas generate many other ideas which then promote more ideas resulting in unbelievable creativity and innovation.

Unfortunately, the opposite is also true.

When we are upset at someone or something, it is tempting to voice our complaints to friends or loved ones hoping to enlist their support in validating our feelings. A friend will usually be glad to offer that support out of love and compassion.

If these two people continue to hash over the grievance, each building on the other's negative energy, we have the same exponential multiplication of energy as in the other examples. Only this time, that energy is negative. By the time the bashing session is over, both (or all) people involved are convinced of the absolute validity of the grievance and the total villainy of the person(s) or institutions that caused it.

An example of this energy of grievance was presented to me when I walked in on a conversation between two friends discussing the behavior of a recent houseguest.

To me, the behavior in question was not evil or even disrespectful, but rather suggested someone who perhaps lacked self-confidence in the situation and/or felt like she didn't belong in the otherwise tight-knit group. The other party to the discussion had also noticed that this person was somewhat reticent around her. Both friends had confided their observations separately to me before this incident, so I was aware of the context and their feelings when I came upon their discussion.

When I got there, this conversation had obviously been going on for a while, and by that time this poor houseguest was practically the devil personified.

What started out as behaviors that at first had been simply perceived as unusual, had now been catapulted into gross disrespect and disdain, with the two friends being the victims of this obviously vicious person.

What began as a discussion about why a person may have acted differently than expected, had now grown into a full-blown catalogue of perceived insults and injuries.

In allowing their negative energy to resonate and expand out of proportion, the two friends had missed the opportunity to bring compassionate insight into the situation, and in so doing, built up a false perception of the houseguest that could not easily be undone.

This is the power of energetic exchange, both the positive and the negative, both equally powerful, but with opposite results.

As I pondered this exchange and sought to cool it down, I couldn't help thinking about how this dynamic works on a larger scale.

Resonating negative energy is what makes mobs so dangerous. Even mild mannered individuals who are never violent, can get caught up in negative energy escalation and become raging monsters. The larger the group, the more energy there is to multiply, and as it does, it affects all those with whom it comes in contact.

Other examples which come to mind are group bullying, gang rape and fraternity hazing. which are all the more tragic because many of the perpetrators are otherwise peaceful, sane and caring people. Because they did not understand the powerful lure of negative group energy, they allowed themselves to be caught up in something they will regret for the rest of their lives.

I see this same dynamic working on the national level as well, where political feelings are running high on both sides, and it seems there is no common ground. Each side retreats to its own bubble and delights in the resonating negative energy to be found there.

One example is the hatefest surrounding Hillary Clinton in the 2016 U.S. election. At that time, I did some extensive research to find the origin of the anti-Hillary feeling that was raging even among some long-time Democrats. As hard as I looked, I could find nothing truly substantive that would account for the high level of dislike and disgust. Unfortunately, Hillary's long tenure in public life has allowed any negative energy surrounding her to multiply tenfold, creating an extremely effective negative energy bubble.

Shrewd manipulators can easily ferret out these negative energy bubbles and add fire to the smoke with exaggeration, innuendo and outright fake news.

Now we see the same thing happening with the current President. While Trump is certainly his own worst enemy, the negative energy exchange surrounding him is counter-productive and distracts us from the real issues of the day, and what we want to do about them.

While bashing and trolling are satisfying to the ego because they solidify the righteousness of our opinions, they generate group energy that is dissonant, out of balance and full of friction. This kind of energy destroys rather than creates, deflates rather than inspires, and leaves us falsely complacent.

Remember that negative energy attracts negative energy, and that means the more we become seduced by the lure of trolling or bashing, the more negative energy we attract, and the less positive energy there is for constructive creation.

On the national level, we are robbing ourselves of the energy we need to come together in collaboration to solve our problems. On the personal level, we run the risk of character assassination and victimization rather than trying to access the wisdom needed to understand and heal.

While all of us need to vent from time to time, it is important to understand when enough is enough, and how easily things can get out of control when you allow yourself to be seduced by escalating negative energy.

When you do need to vent, there are constructive ways to do it. The next chapter addresses this issue.

26
Whining With Awareness

Whining has gotten a bad rap, but it doesn't have to be all bad. Everyone has to do it from time to time. If we are going to whine, however, it's good to do it with awareness.

Whining with awareness means understanding what we are doing when we whine, and acknowledging and listening to that part of us that needs to do it.

That part is a younger part, a part of us that needs to be taken care of, needs to have some authority take charge, needs to turn over responsibility to someone who knows the answers and has the resources and the power to take care of the problems or irritations we are experiencing.

That person is the adult you.

This younger part of ourselves, which is sometimes called The Inner Child, is very real and very important. Although it often feels overwhelmed and helpless, it is also the part of us that loves to play, is innocently optimistic and full of love and laughter. When it whines, it wants to be seen, acknowledged and reassured.

Between the lines however, there is often much more information. If we listen closely we can learn a lot. It is only by listening to our own whining that we can begin to understand where the real problem lies.

Unfortunately, sometimes we use whining not just as a way to be recognized in the moment and to gain insight, but as a way to continue to get attention. When this happens our problems actually become the means to an end, so we are not really interested in solving them. As long as we have problems to whine about, people will continue to pay attention to us, and we can continue stealing energy from them.

If discussing our problems with others never results in any solution, and/or we find ourselves whining about the same thing over and over, then we are not whining with awareness, and our friends may drop away because they realize on some level they are being used.

It's human nature to blame someone else when we feel helpless, and at the same time expect, hope, want, demand that someone else "fix" the problem.

As children we were helpless, and depended on our parents to take care of things. But as adults, many of us have replaced responsible parents with others in authority; the church, the medical community, the government, the banks, the boss, the union, etc. Helplessness thus brings much anger, some directed at those whose "fault" it is, and some directed at those who should be able to "fix" the problem but are not doing it.

When we are angry at a person (spouse, relative, co-worker), we often try to force them to change, and then get even angrier when that doesn't work. When we are angry at an institution or government, (as so many are right now) we find that most institutions today are themselves in a process of decay and breakdown.

Whether we are angry at a person or an institution for either causing or not solving our problems, we can only get angrier and more frustrated, because neither the other person, nor today's institutions can solve our problems.

The only real power we have to change anything, is to change ourselves.

Once we take responsibility for solving our own problems, we can listen with awareness to our own whining. By listening with awareness, we probe the underbelly of the whale.

A client recently needed to whine about her husband's temper. After venting for a while about the latest episode, she began to realize that her husband's temper had forced her to learn how to get angry and stand up for herself, something she had been forbidden to do as a child.

After feeling powerless in the face of his wrath for many years, she finally taught herself how to be angry in a constructive way, allowing her energy to be strong and forceful but without vengeance or hostility. As she talked about having learned this skill, she also realized that her husband's temper had improved tremendously since she had started to stand up for herself, and this latest incident was in fact, now an isolated occurrence.

While she really needed to whine, she was also able to listen to herself, observing her words as they came out of her mouth, gaining insights as she continued to vent. She needed to allow her Inner Child to complain, but she also brought her adult self and soul into the picture by listening with awareness. Her adult-self acknowledged her child-self and supported her, while her soul brought forth the wisdom needed to understand the situation.

What started out as a feeling of helplessness, evolved into a profound realization about how she really did know how to handle the situation constructively.

What started as anger at her husband, ended with deep appreciation for him, not only for how much he had changed (because she had changed), but also how many gifts they had given each other in their marriage.

27
Everyday Blessings

So often we witness emotional or physical pain, or even heartbreak and tragedy, and wish there was something we could do.

Well, there is.

A blessing is simply a transfer of loving energy, an energy gift, with no agenda and no expectation of anything in return. It is simple, profound and incredibly effective, and can be done in the blink of an eye, even from great distances. All it takes is your intention to transfer positive energy (love, honor and respect) from the depth of your heart to another person.

And you don't need to be confronted with heartbreak or tragedy to prove to yourself how powerful this gift is.

The next time you're in the grocery store, take a deep breath and bring your attention entirely to the present moment. Bring yourself to a place of gratitude and appreciation for all that is around you – your ability to see, feel, smell the richness of physical life. In this way, you can release all the distractions that usually keep us from being truly focused on our interactions with others. In this way, you can interact from the heart.

In this state, you can look the clerk in the eye when you say, "Thank you", and send him heartfelt blessings for his work and his connection with you, no matter how brief or satisfactory.

Then notice the reaction.

Most often, when you do this, you will see him do a double take, and really connect with you too, if only for an instant. Usually, he will gift you back with a smile, even when there had been a frown before. For a brief instant, true connection has been made, a blessing has been given and received, and that one brief instant can really change a person's day (and yours too).

Think about all those times we use pointless fillers in our interactions with others. When we say "Have a good day", or "Thank you" or "Good to see you" and put no real energy behind what we are saying.

When you load these words with heartfelt blessings that really convey energetically what the words are supposed to mean, watch how people light up around you.

Experience how love, honor and respect transform people and relationships. And the gift comes right back to you when you realize how such a little thing can have such a big impact on others' lives.

Once you have experienced the impact of everyday blessings, you will then be ready to apply your newfound ability to larger areas. You will know beyond doubt that your energy gifts can help people who are experiencing despair and tragedy. Your blessings are not limited by time or space – you can send them from great distances. You can even send them to groups, regions or nations that are experiencing hard times and chaos.

Just remember that blessings have no agendas, even positive ones like peace or healing. They are true gifts that allow the recipient to use the energy in whatever way is needed at the moment.

Section Six

Relationship With Self

28

Daring to Love Yourself

Truly loving yourself takes a lot of courage and resolve.

Why? Because it goes against much of what we have been taught.

It is in society's' best interest to establish cultural norms that teach us to put others before ourselves. Self-love can therefore be quite challenging because it goes against what culture demands. For women especially, putting others' needs before our own is a hard role to break out of.

We all strive to be "good" people, and those who care for others before themselves have been culturally defined as being "good" people. If we choose to care for ourselves first, then it's hard not to think of ourselves (even unconsciously) as selfish or "bad".

But trying to define our value by how much we love others or care for them is just another way to massage our egos and prevent the unconditional acceptance of our whole being.

The first step in loving ourselves is exploring our true identity, that is, defining who we are and what we want to accomplish in life without the input of society, culture, friends and family.

So much of what we feel, think, believe and say, is not really ours. It comes from the expectations of other people and culture (in the form of TV, books, movies and the internet). We have assimilated all these expectations as our own without even realizing it because we depend on this input for validation.

When we claim our true identity and rely on only ourselves for validation, we often find ourselves flying in the face of cultural norms.

Given the difficulty this poses, why would we want to undertake this awesome task?

First, you can only really love others if you love yourself. This is certainly not a new or original thought. But why is it so?

If I don't truly love, accept and appreciate myself, with all my warts and selfishness and other negative traits, whatever I do for others (no matter how apparently selfless or noble), will always have a personal agenda attached to it. If I do not love and accept myself completely, I will always be looking for validation from others.

Doing "good" deeds is one way of getting validation, but it has an agenda nonetheless. If I don't get the validation I am looking for, I can become jaded and bitter and soon fall into victimhood.

If I do get the validation I need, it is at best only fleeting and fragile since it is entirely dependent on the whims of others.

It is only when we are completely comfortable in our own being that we can be of true service to others. Service then becomes a gift that has no agenda or personal need attached to it, and is based entirely on the passionate expression of our souls.

Second, loving yourself is the only way to attain true freedom. We think of "freedom" as not being physically confined. But even if we are physically "free" we are almost always culturally confined.

This is not to say that many of society's rules and structures are not valid ways of ensuring fair and safe human interactions. But when you truly love yourself and need no outside validation, you are free to decide for yourself how you want to live your life. You can then create your own moral compass based on treating others the way you treat yourself.

Are we not all inspired by those who are so complete within themselves that they can defy convention and follow the path of their heart wherever it leads despite criticism and controversy? Are we not moved to tears when we see how compassionately and tenderly they treat themselves while the world may be heaping judgment on their shoulders?

But as much as we might admire these people, being around them is often not easy, because loving yourself means not letting others suck your energy. People who love themselves will not allow others to steal their energy by any means. They do not tolerate victimhood, complaining or negative attitudes.

Loving yourself also means being absolutely honest with yourself, and therefore honest with others too, in the gentlest way possible

It means establishing a fair and equal energy exchange with those you choose to call your friends. Although you will still treat those who are infringing on your boundaries with the same compassion with which you treat yourself, neither do you allow yourself to be drawn into other people's dramas. You can simply gracefully withdraw your physical and energetic presence.

Loving ourselves demands new definitions of how we want to be in service. If we no longer allow others to steal our energy in return for validation, how do we focus our loving energy outwards?

We do this by being able to bestow the same honor, respect and appreciation we feel for ourselves, on everyone, even those who seem never to get enough. Just as we are honest with ourselves, we are honest with others to the degree they are able to hear it. We choose what we want to give, when we want to give it, and how much we want to give according to our own standards and an honest appraisal of how much good we are actually doing.

However, it *does* takes courage and daring to do this.

It takes guts to defy conventional expectations and rely solely on self-validation. It is truly a challenge to foster that deep self-appreciation that encompasses all your warts as well as your brilliance, and then act on it in the world.

29

How to Love Yourself 101:
Learn from your Dog! (or Cat)

Do you ever wonder why our pets love us unconditionally?

I'm amazed by how much my dog worships me. It's almost embarrassing, so I tend to dismiss it as something weird about dogs and question no more. But my daughter's cat adores her too. Hmmmmm??? Maybe they know something we don't.

We dismiss our pets' love for us because they are, after all, just "dumb" animals, a product of the natural world without the cognitive ability to know what sh**s we really are.

But that's just it! They ARE a product of the natural world and as such, a reflection of it. Perhaps they are trying to tell us that the natural world, and in fact, the whole of the universe, loves us unconditionally, just as our pets do.

Once animals establish an energetic bond with a human, they take on a sacred responsibility to show us the unconditional love and high esteem all creation has for us.

Like all sentient beings our pets participate in the polarity of the physical world. They learn as young animals what is dangerous and what is not. But they don't seem to put polarity in absolute boxes like humans do. They never judge, but instead use discernment. They keep away from us when we are angry, but never waver in their love, coming back the minute we calm down.

Humans, on the other hand, have pushed duality to its limits, choosing judgment rather than discernment. We place things on one side or the other, good or bad, black or white, and these categories then become absolute. We then apply these judgments to ourselves as well as to others.

We strive to be "good" but know we fall short on many counts. So we either hide this knowledge from ourselves, or shame ourselves in hope of getting rid of the offending characteristics or behavior. In order to be "good" we cannot love or value anything that is flawed, which includes ourselves.

What if good and bad were not absolutes?

What if this was something we just made up because it was easier that way?

What if our brains and consciousness were now developed enough to recognize duality as only a mental concept, not part of an absolute reality?

Our souls, just like our pets, know that polarity is just a tool to help keep us safe in the physical world and grow our consciousness. The ability to discern opposites was never meant to freeze us into the stiff boxes our emotions seem to demand.

While most of us rely on other humans to give us value and self-worth, we forget that other people see duality as absolute too. Other humans are extremely unreliable as reflections of love and value. What they give they can also take away. Deep down we know this, so we can never get enough love and esteem from other humans.

When you learn to love and value yourself, no one can strip that from you, and you can always create all you need.

The unconditional love of your dog or cat is not strange or unusual or to be marveled at. Their esteem is a reflection of a higher reality they know instinctively.

Learn to see yourself through their eyes. You are a whole person with many facets, each with its own blessings and curses. This is what it means to be human. These facets are what you must have to experience all of physical life in its entirety.

Our pets are here to remind us that the universe

loves and values us just for being courageous enough to come to Earth and struggle with the challenge of having to forget our eternal origins. We are loved and cherished just for being here.

Pets know this and reflect it back to us every day. We can learn a lot from them.

30

Transforming the Inner Critic

One of the greatest obstacles to learning self-love is the Inner Critic—you know—that voice in your head that's always catching you off guard, finding something negative about everything you do.

The Inner Critic is one of a constellation of voices or sub-personalities that make up your individualized self. It is one of the energy patterns you created when you were a child to help navigate the physical world.

Believe it or not, your Inner Critic loves you and wants to serve you. As your creation, it is intense and often toxic because it takes its job so seriously. That job is to keep others from criticizing you by getting there first. In this way, it protects you from the harsh judgments of those around you, and any possible harm that might come as a result.

While the Inner Critic is intense and focused, it is not very creative. It has learned how to get your attention from early authority figures in your life.

If you listen closely to the voice of your Inner Critic, you can probably hear the echoes of people in your childhood who also felt the need to teach you the way of the world by criticizing you – a parent, grandparent, teacher, coach, minister or priest. They probably felt that the more negative the criticism, the more likely it was to get your attention.

Harsh criticism is a kind of emotional and energetic abuse. It is a force that doesn't hurt physically, but it is oh-so painful emotionally. It can cripple our spirit, robbing us of self-confidence, the ability to move forward, and passion for life.

Today, at the beginning of the 21st century, we are starting to realize that force is not an appropriate or effective way to get human beings to do anything. Toxic criticism is a kind of verbal force that is automatically met with resistance and denial.

Rather than deter us from the criticized action, we are more likely to show our independence by engaging in it. Nonetheless, if that criticism is repeated often enough, we begin to believe it in spite of our conscious efforts not to let it affect us.

Many people try to solve this problem by attempting to fight the Inner Critic, to banish it from consciousness, to ignore or resist it. This strategy is not effective because the more you ignore it or try to get rid of it, the louder it becomes – a natural resistance to your harsh treatment, to your own resistance.

In addition, the Inner Critic is a necessary and vital part of every personality and does have an important job, so you really don't want to be without it.

Fortunately, it is possible to transform your Inner Critic, (as well as any other problematic sub-personality), by teaching it to be more compassionate and constructive. Since you created this part of yourself as a child, you can now recreate it, much like you reprogram your computer when the program you are using is out-of-date.

Your Inner Critic says what it says, simply because it knows no other way of carrying out its job, and it desperately wants to serve you and do its job well. If it is no longer serving you constructively, then it is up to you to show it how it can do its job more successfully.

You can dialogue with your Inner Critic just as if it were a real person as long as you approach it with the same energy you want from it, compassion, understanding and unconditional love. You must set the example.

The next time your inner Critic speaks harshly to you, stop for a moment and really listen to what it's saying. Do you even agree that this issue is still true or important to you? Since criticism is often a reflection of people in your early life, it may be completely outdated. If it is not important or even true, simply inform your Inner Critic that this issue is no longer valid and shouldn't be broached again.

If the issue *is* important, let your Inner Critic know that harsh criticism results in defensiveness and causes the person being criticized to rebel against, or resist the advice or admonition.

Think about how a kind, loving parent or wise master might deliver the same information in a compassionate, constructive way. Then suggest this kind of approach to your Inner Critic.

Taming your Inner Critic takes time and thought. Since it is habituated to using certain language, you will have to be constantly aware of the need to lovingly reprogram how it speaks to you. The more consistent you are, and the more you pay attention to the reprogramed advice, the faster your Inner Critic will learn the new program.

Transforming your Inner Critic makes life much easier, more joyful and productive, and can also change your relationships with others. When you learn to treat yourself with love and compassion, it spills over into everything you do.

31

Waves of Our Lives

When we become aware of energy as an important part of everyday reality, the wave metaphor can help us understand many things about our lives that may have been perplexing before.

Waves are defined not by their location in space as a discrete entity, but can only be described by wavelength (distance between crests), amplitude (distance between the crest and trough) and frequency (the number of times a crest passes a particular point in a second). In other words, a wave is a vibration that goes up and down in cycles.

Even matter is a form of energy just moving in slow motion. In the material world we have cycles that reflect the wave patterns of subatomic energy, like day and night, and summer and winter. We have biorhythms in our bodies. We have bull and bear stock markets that follow each other in irregular cycles, but cycles nonetheless.

Recognizing cycles as natural and necessary to everyday life can bring greater understanding to many aspects life. But there is one cycle that is particularly important to many of us on Earth right now. This is the cycle of psychological expansion and contraction.

The low end of this cycle is what has been mistakenly called depression.

Depression has become a cash cow for pharmaceutical companies that have both capitalized on, and promoted, the idea that depression is pathology.

However, most depression is not pathology. It is a natural and necessary part of a cycle.

There are times in our lives when we naturally feel expansive. We enjoy life and want to share our excitement with those around us. We reach out to other people with joy and laughter, and feel productive in whatever we are engaged in, whether it be school work, our jobs or careers, family life, creative expression or community volunteering.

But inevitably, after a period of expansiveness, we become unbalanced physically, mentally and/or spiritually.

We are so outwardly oriented that we fail to notice that we may have hurt some feelings, made some mistakes in our work, or neglected our creative or spiritual side. We may have been so physically active we have not given our bodies time to rest. We may have overexerted our minds to the point of exhaustion. We may have become bored with our jobs because we are no longer challenged and need new opportunities.

Becoming unbalanced after a time of expansion is natural and necessary for continued physical, psychological and spiritual growth.

We learn more and are stretched far beyond our usual comfort limits by imbalances like "mistakes" and "failures" than by our successes. The ego glories in success, but when we are successful we tend to repeat the same strategies over and over. This behavior may be viewed as productive and successful in the outer world, but it can lead to boredom and stagnation in our inner world.

When we become unbalanced we contract and become "depressed". Although this low end of the cycle certainly doesn't feel great, it is an important adaptive mechanism designed to alert us to the fact that there is an imbalance.

Think of the symptoms of depression.

We feel lethargic. We don't want to go out, or be around people. We have no energy or passion for even the things that interested us before. We feel awful and know that something is "wrong" but often can't put our finger on what it is. Or, many times, we know what is wrong but we adopt a victim attitude and conclude that an abusive boss or a boring job is just something to bear and not something we can do anything about.

Quiet time and self-reflection can provide the undisturbed time needed to notice the imbalance, and/or the insight into the action we must take to right the imbalance. Our bodies are providing just the kind of environment for that to happen - alone time away from usual activities so we can engage in thought and self-reflection.

Unfortunately, the many antidepressants available today, and the ease of getting them, have allowed us to sweep these imbalances under the rug so we can continue as before.

And guess what? Drugs just numb the pain.

What is worse, drugs prevent us from paying attention to the energetic information we are receiving. Antidepressants actually make the problem worse because they make it possible to continue to treat the problem like a physical illness without really dealing with the underlying imbalances themselves. Consequently, what often starts out as mild depression soon becomes severe and chronic.

Depression is the body/soul's message that something is out of balance, and you can and must do something about it, even if you don't think you know how.

Out of balance energy is stuck energy that is holding you back and causing you to stagnate. Depression is a sign that it is time to move on, to stretch your wings and develop potentials you didn't know you had. It is asking you to sit quietly and think about your situation, asking yourself what is wrong and how to move ahead.

A simple intention to solve the problem(s) will start the process.

Even if you have no idea what the problem(s) might be, it is still important to decide on a first step.

This could be talking to a trusted counselor or friend about what might be unbalanced in your life. Enlisting the aid of another often provides a more objective perspective that can help us see beyond the stuckness.

Exercise is also an excellent way of encouraging energy flow in the body, which will, in turn, help us feel more positive about our ability to move ahead psychologically. We know that exercise releases endorphins in the brain that help us feel better and have a more positive outlook on life.

Maybe you do have an idea of what the problem may be, but don't think you can do anything about it.

However, your soul in its infinite wisdom, knows you better than your conscious self, and it gives information only when you are ready for it. If you are experiencing depression because of an imbalance in your life, then you are ready to move beyond the problem. You wouldn't be experiencing these feelings if you were not capable of moving forward even though it may at first seem scary.

It is also important to remember that depression and grief, although they feel similar, are not the same thing. When something important changes in our lives, we must grieve for what has gone.

Loss is part of the cycle of life, so is grief.

There is no way around grief. The only way forward is through it. If you don't allow yourself to fully experience your grief, it will turn into stuck energy as well, and continue to be a problem long past the time it would normally have eased.

Even though the physical world around us seems static or fixed, and we yearn for the familiar and stable, the natural state of energy is flow.

Since we are energy beings, our natural state is also movement and flow. Waves of energy go up and down, and so does life. If we embrace these natural cycles rather than resist them, we can move forward with ease and grace.

32

What is True Love?
A Radical Concept

True love is most often associated with romantic love. But is romantic love really "love" at all?

Romantic love is a result of attraction, and it's certainly a powerful force. It happens when two people feel that the other completes them.

We all have potentials that are not yet developed and expressed, but are just waiting to break out and evolve. When we meet another who has already developed these potentials, we are immediately attracted and inspired. When this other person reflects not just one, but many of our undeveloped potentials, and that person also sees many of his or her undeveloped potentials in us, then we fall in love.

Those who are "in love" seem to walk on air, they seem truly lit up with happiness. They feel finally complete because the relationship has filled holes that seemed empty and needed filling before, first by validating lovability, and second, by supplying these undeveloped potentials in fully developed form.

We often characterize this state of bliss as "true love".

Before our modern times, the partnership that was formed by this situation was the best possible outcome for both people. Men and women were attracted to each other because they each embodied potentials that might have been realized by the other, but were usually not allowed to develop because of cultural norms.

Men had certain roles and women had other roles, and it was highly unusual and socially problematic for one gender to infringe on the other's territory.

But the social climate today has changed to the point where men and women can develop potentials that were formerly reserved for only one gender. For example, men are developing their ability to be nurturing by playing larger and larger roles in the lives of their children, and women are working outside the home developing the more masculine qualities needed to excel in the workforce.

Of course, not all of what inspires us in another has to do with gender roles.

The old saying is that "opposites attract", and this seems especially true for relationships. For example, an introverted, reflective person is attracted to someone outgoing and vivacious. Eventually the introverted person may become more outgoing as he learns social skills from his mate, while his partner may realize the advantages of a more reflective outlook on life.

Or a rugged outdoorsman may be attracted to a cleanliness obsessed, hairdryer fixated woman. If each is open to why they were attracted in the first place, the man could well become more organized and tidy while the women might discover a growing appreciation for the outdoors, something she never would have experienced had her lover not introduced her to it.

Today, a healthy relationship is one where both people will learn from one another and eventually develop many of the potentials that were formerly only fully expressed by one or the other.

Ironically, while this sounds great on the surface, it often brings tremendous problems for the partnership. If enough of these potentials are fully realized, the result may well be that the couple no longer feels romantically attracted.

Although this situation can be viewed as a positive outcome from a higher perspective, it is usually seen as a huge crisis for those involved. Since romantic love is generally thought to be the glue that holds the relationship together, its loss threatens the belief systems upon which the partnership is based.

Often one or the other may seek a new romance outside the relationship, causing much anguish. Or one or both may start finding fault with the other in order to explain why things are not the way they were. Some may just decide that the relationship is not working any more and part company.

However, this crisis is also an opportunity to move into a more mature kind of love, a true and unconditional love, a state where we no longer "need" one another for completion or validation, but instead choose to give our love freely with no strings or needs attached.

Being able to offer this kind of love depends on whether a person has grown into wholeness, has achieved a sovereignty in his or her own being where potentials have been developed, and is able to love themselves unconditionally. In this case, energy and validation from others is no longer needed.

This kind of love can be offered whether or not two people choose to stay together. It can also be offered by one person to the other, even if the other is not there yet, since it needs nothing in return.

If both people have arrived at this point together, the romantic attraction of need and personal growth can be replaced by an attraction based on the existential duality of separation and unity.

We choose union for a brief time of ecstasy, and

then separate to experience once again our own unique and individual being. Since we need nothing from the other, we are free to give all of ourselves, while in return experiencing the whole being of the other. Perhaps this is the real "true love".

Love without need—a truly radical concept.

Section Seven
Soul Dynamics

33

Energy Dimension Helpers

When we begin to realize that the physical world is only one aspect of reality, the possibility of unseen, energetic "helpers" starts to make sense. It is possible that many of the strange things that may have happened to us over the years could be the direct result of energetic help from other realms.

What about that almost car accident that came so close you couldn't believe you actually drove away intact? What about the hard fall on the ice that should have broken bones but didn't? What about the boiling pot left forgotten on the stove that should have burned the house down except that the burner mysteriously turned off. We can't explain these apparent miracles and strange coincidences by looking only at the physical laws of cause and effect.

There is, in fact, a whole host of helpers in the energy dimension that can affect our lives in many ways.

The primary among them is the soul, which is eternal, and the repository of infinite wisdom and all potentials both past and future. The soul is both a part of us here on Earth, and an anchor for us in the larger multidimensional cosmos. It very much wants to work with us to co-create our lives and our reality here in the physical realm.

Nonetheless, the soul is respectful of us as physical beings and will not impose itself on our free will choices.

It is therefore necessary for each of us to make a conscious choice to invite the soul into our lives, and develop a co-creative partnership. When we do this, help is much more available, simply because we asked for it, and we will start noticing that help more and more.

Even before making this commitment, there is still help, both before and/or after we ask for it. Guardian angels, elementals, plant and place devas and spirit guides are always there for us and can help us until we become aware of the soul, and are able to form a true partnership.

Guardian angels watch over us and help keep us on the planet, but they can't interact. They are always present and help us even when we are completely unaware that we have multidimensional help.

There are also elemental spirits like fairies and elves that take care of plants and minerals, as well as special guardian spirits that look after buildings (like your house) and specific tracts of land. Gardens have garden devas that help coordinate what you want to create with the elementals that look after the plants.

When we begin to wake up spiritually, we are usually still looking for an authority of some kind, and also need to be able to interact in a familiar way.

Spirit guides, who are often wise beings who once lived on Earth, can fill this role because they understand how hard it is to be a human, and can also more readily communicate in ways that resemble human language and behavior.

Their role is to gently wean us from the need for any authority other than our own, help us learn how to love ourselves unconditionally, and teach us how to communicate energetically.

Spirit guides come in many different metaphorical forms.

They can be animals, angels, ancestors, Native Americans, Shamans, Zen monks, beloved relatives who have passed over, or wise beings that are somewhat amorphous. They will appear in whatever form is the most meaningful for you at the time.

It is important to note, however, that not all disincarnate entities are wise beings capable of being spirit guides. We need to be discerning in our choice of spirit guides and helpers just as we need to be discerning in our choice of teachers and mentors in the physical realm.

Below is a list of what to look for in a teacher or guide in any dimension.

1. Is loving and compassionate, never judgmental.
2. Commands attention but does not demand obedience.
3. Never looks for ego enhancement or asserts dominion over others.
4. Leads us beyond our own ego because they have already gone beyond theirs.
5. Never takes advantage either physically, emotionally, sexually, financially, spiritually, or in any other way.
6. Discourages dependence by fostering a relationship of equality and co-creation.
7. Empowers by encouraging us to rely on our own resources, to see ourselves in new ways and to make our own decisions.
8. Encourages wholeness and accepts both light and dark.
9. Always leads directly or indirectly back to ourselves, to our own connection to wisdom.
10. Is transient.

Since the purpose of a guide is to help us grow, a guide's success means that the need for that guide will diminish over time. A person who is experiencing spiritual growth will move on to new guides and eventually to few and very transient guides and then to the soul itself.

A guide represents the energy of assistance, and will often make its presence known through repetitious experiences, symbols or synchronicities.

Guides are available to help in your spiritual growth, but are not necessarily problems solvers. They will never interfere with your free will, and will usually not give you advice on how you should live your life or what paths you should take or not take. They know that you will get where you are going no matter what path you take, and whatever path you take has important information for you.

Spirit guides are not permanent. Since one of their jobs is to help you develop and trust your own wisdom, they are loath to encourage dependency by hanging around indefinitely.

After my first spirit guide, I have had many others, some in the form of animal guides, and some in other forms depending on where I was at that time. Ultimately, I learned to love myself and to see spirit guides and ascended masters as equals, not authority figures. My spirit guides also taught me the language of metaphor and symbol which prepared me for direct communication with my soul.

Think back on your life and count all the miracles and strange occurrences that cannot be explained. The more you think back, the more you'll remember. We are far more loved and cared for than we could ever imagine.

34

Getting to Know Your Soul

Did you know that your soul "speaks" to you all the time?

In the rushing waters, the gentle breezes, the trees sighing in the wind, the soul calms the heart and offers unconditional love to all who will listen and feel.

We have all experienced these times of deep unity with all that is, and with that part of us that is always connected. But that sense of sacred connection is only the first step in getting to know your soul. The soul "speaks" in many other ways as well, ways that often do not involve sound and almost never make sense logically. Unfortunately we are therefore quick to dismiss or ignore valuable information coming from a very deep and wise part of ourselves.

Not only is this communication often dismissed because it is not verbal or logically explainable, but also because we don't believe that any part of us personally could produce this kind of wisdom. Most of us don't really love ourselves, nor trust that we might have a source of inner wisdom available to us at all times.

In addition, Newtonian physics teaches us to question the reality of anything that does not lend itself to scientific inquiry.

The soul is not visible or tangible, nor has anyone figured out how to prove its existence through scientific experimentation. Therefore, it does not exist scientifically, which means that many of us dismiss it entirely.

The advent of quantum physics offers new life for the concept of soul, however. Quantum physics deals with invisible, non-physical concepts such as quarks and black holes.

It considers the reality of an item by how it affects those things that are physical and tangible rather than by whether it can be seen or detected by the eye or by technology. It posits numerous added dimensions beyond our known four and predicts scientific outcomes based on the assumption that all things are connected at the quantum level.

As people become more comfortable looking at

reality as composed of both matter and energy, the concept of soul becomes more real, more present and more accessible.

At the beginning of the 21st Century, we are ready for a new way of understanding the soul itself, as well as its immediate availability and vast potential. Now the soul is real and it speaks to us all the time. It speaks in a code that we have long forgotten but which is right at our fingertips, begging to be interpreted and understood.

Once we understand that code, we are amazed to find that information is all around us, and that we are always in the midst of a constant flow of wisdom available simply by asking and observing.

The soul speaks energetically and poetically, not logically. It communicates in whole thoughts and images rather than linear language. It arranges symbolic information through synchronicities, and through metaphorical language and images.

It loves the landscape of dreams and often makes itself known there. It sees our lives from a higher perspective that is impossible to reach without its help. It loves us unconditionally and seeks conscious recognition, communication and co-creation. It is eternal.

Where is the soul?

Because it is not material, it can reside both inside and outside us at the same time. It is multidimensional and omnipresent.

The part outside is able to maintain a higher, more expansive perspective because it participates in the divine connection of all creation. The part inside us coordinates our physical, emotional, mental and spiritual energy when allowed to do so. We are surrounded and infused by our souls at all times.

Even though the soul is always with us, we do not usually recognize its language because we have not been taught how to detect or interpret it. But this knowledge is available, and like any skill, the more we practice, the easier it is.

Learning to work with the soul rather than at cross-purposes will change your life.

Instead of constantly trying to swim up river, working with your soul allows you to enter the divine flow of life that moves you along with much less effort and resistance. Gaining a soul perspective brings a sense of purpose and understanding not available any other way.

Experiencing soul love gives you a source of divine energy and a real sense of how to love yourself.

35
Soul Language

It is truly unfortunate that most of us learn about metaphor and symbol only in advanced literature and art classes.

Consequently, we in Western culture think of language and communication only as the linear, logical form of spoken and written language we use every day. While indigenous cultures have always understood the importance of metaphor and symbol in their communications with other dimensions, only artists work with these marvelous tools in Western culture.

Our ignorance in this area is one of the major reasons much soul communication goes unnoticed.

The language of the soul is imaginative rather

than rational. It is interpreted in the right side of the brain rather than the left. It is associative rather than logical. It is spatial rather than linear and figurative rather than literal. The language of the soul is energetic, and almost all energetic language is metaphorical.

The difference between metaphoric language and linear language is that metaphors and symbols have many meanings rather than just one. They are not linear in that many meanings may be piled on top of one another in layers, or organized in a timeless fashion where there is no beginning, middle and end.

Metaphors and symbols are associative rather than logical; rather than being related by cause and effect, two things may be meaningfully associated just because they happened at the same time or are in the same space.

The beauty of this kind of communication is that it can be highly personal and individualized, not one size fits all.

One prime example of this versatility is the Christian Bible, which is so full of metaphoric language that it has allowed Christianity to spawn hundreds or even thousands of different sects depending on individual interpretations of this important spiritual book. The symbolic nature of Biblical verse allows for many meanings and interpretations according to the needs of the times and of the different groups of people living in those times and places.

This characteristic is both an advantage and a disadvantage.

It is an advantage because it allows each of us to get just the precise information we need. It may seem like a disadvantage, however, in that we have to work much harder to gain the information that is presented. Ironically, that for which we have to work hard is usually much more meaningful and important to us.

The soul communicates in two ways, indirectly and directly.

Indirect communication often comes in the form of synchronicities or meaningful coincidences. These symbolic life events are messages from the soul suggesting ways to grow, changes in direction, affirmation or clarification of a choice made, or just plain help when you need it.

Since I live in a rural area, synchronistic events for me often have to do with animals. Indigenous people have always given animals symbolic meanings. There are many books and oracle decks that can help us familiarize ourselves with the metaphoric information each animal carries.

In my case, I have many squirrels on my property to which I usually pay no attention. I see perhaps hundreds of squirrels a day, so normally they carry no information.

However, if a squirrel sits on my office windowsill and refuses to leave, even after vigorous pounding on the window, I know he has a message for me.

Squirrel energy has to do with gathering and saving, and also with clutter and hoarding, so I assume this pesky window visitor is asking me to review my consumer habits. Either I do not have enough of something I need, or I need to de-clutter and release either physically or energetically. It is up to me to interpret what is the correct message for me at that point in time.

You can recognize synchronistic events by their out-of-the-ordinariness. If something happens in your life that is unusual, weird, abnormally difficult or easy, repetitious, illogical or miraculous, it is information from the soul.

Metaphoric associations and expressions, oracle decks, and your own energetic senses can help you interpret the information.

When you ask yourself questions about the meaning of this event for you, pay attention to the energetic charge your body feels with each question. Usually a "yes" answer will bring a positively charged feeling, and a "no" answer will make you feel uncomfortable or just empty.

Another form of indirect communication is dreams. Most of our dreams are just stories of alternative ways to experience the world. We dream and forget them, or dream and remember only briefly and then forget.

But every once in awhile, we get a dream that seems so real and so intense that it's easy to remember, and so vivid we know it holds some important information. Dreams of this kind can be interpreted using your knowledge of metaphor and symbol as well as by looking for energetic charge, much the same as you would interpret synchronicities.

1. Who or what were the primary characters in the dream, and with what do you associate them?
2. What were the repetitious, unusual or outstandingly weird parts of the dream and how do they relate to your current situation?
3. If there are animals or archetypal figures (mother, crone, king, angel, etc.), what is their archetypal meaning and your association with that meaning?
4. Pretend each of the characters in the dream is as aspect of yourself and see what associations and feelings that brings to you.

Usually these dreams come unbidden. But it is also possible to ask for a dream to help you with a problem. In this case, a dream can be a direct method of soul communication, that is, one that you initiate rather than one the soul itself brings to you.

I once had a severe pain in my right arm that

wouldn't go away. Medical people could find no cause and I was left with no relief. So, I asked my soul to send a dream to help me understand why I was experiencing this pain.

That night I dreamed I was riding a horse bareback with only a halter and a short rope to guide him by. I had to lean out over the horse's neck to grasp the rope because it was so short, and that effort put my arm in a very awkward and uncomfortable position.

At one point, the horse became tangled in some wire and I had to get off him to remove the wire. After I did so, he ran away. I was devastated and thought I'd lost him. I didn't think I'd ever be able to get him back. But I called him anyway, and was surprised when he came right to me.

I was then in a quandary because he was quite large, and I had no saddle or stirrup to help mount him. After few a moments frustration, I decided to ask him to be still while I got on since I knew it would take a while. Again, he was very patient and waited until I got settled before moving.

After all this incredible cooperation on the horse's part, I wondered if I could just ask him to do what I wanted rather than using a rein. I tried it, and again he complied beautifully. Then I woke up.

When looking for an interpretation I remembered that a horse is a symbol of power, especially personal power.

Beverly Crane, PhD.

The dream was telling me that I was holding my personal power "on a short rope", afraid it would get away from me and I would abuse it. The pain in my arm was a message from my soul that it was time to let go. I didn't need to "rein in" my personal power because I could now command it responsibly, simply by conscious intention. A day later, the pain in my arm vanished.

Through mastering metaphor and symbol, paying attention to energy signals, and noticing the weird and wonderful synchronistic events in our lives, we can learn the language of the soul.

36
Connecting With the Soul

Once we become aware of our soul, and consciously choose to connect to it, we can engage in direct communication, which is when you initiate contact (just as I did in the "short rein" dream) by asking for help.

You can signal your readiness to work with your soul by creating a ritual, or just by simple request. Making that request means you are ready to try to see things from a soul perspective and to listen to the wisdom that the soul imparts.

After inviting your soul to work with you, you can request direct contact in meditation, ask for a dream, or use oracle decks of various kinds, which are excellent tools for learning how to think symbolically.

Direct soul contact is greatly enhanced by a meditation practice.

Calming, emptying and even bypassing the mind is often necessary before the soul can enter. The mind is full of fears and anxiety which tend to block connecting energy, so it's important to learn to relax and move into the right side of the brain where you can see things from a higher (soul) perspective.

Soul perspective is one of no judgment.

The soul loves you and knows that you are doing the best you can, but that you will nonetheless make many mistakes in those endeavors.

Because it does not judge you, it is hard to make energetic contact with the soul when you still criticize yourself and others harshly. In my experience, direct contact usually does not happen until a person understands the nature of duality and can move beyond the absolute judgments most of us tend to make here on Earth.

Gaining a soul perspective helps you experience true compassion and greater understanding of the human condition. It is therefore important to accept yourself unconditionally, in all your various roles, sub-personalities, shadow and multidimensional aspects.

Meditation is one way to gain higher perspective and practice coming from the heart so that the soul can establish a connection. Meditation is also a place where you can practice pulling your energy back to you (centering) and grounding it.

Grounding your energy puts you in direct contact with the universal energy field which then also allows energy communication (from the soul or other energy contacts such as animals or other people) through that connection.

After relaxing your body and mind, breathe in and imagine your breath pulling your energy back to you. On the out breath, breathe that energy down to the center of your body just below the navel, and then breathe it down further into the ground. Feel your energy going out into the earth like tree roots.

Then breathe your energy back up to your heart center where it continues to gather until it spills out all around you. Now it is time to take most of that energy out through your crown to meet the energy of your soul coming to greet you just above the top of your head. This exercise (Running Energy), will connect you not only to the earth but to the universal energy field that envelops the whole universe.

From this place, you can bathe in the unconditional love your soul has for you. From this place, you can also ask questions and receive answers.

How do you know the information you are getting is from your soul?

1. Communication from the soul will often come through the right side of the brain – through association rather than logic, coincidence rather than cause and effect, metaphor, symbol, poetry and art, rather than reason and logic.

2. Communication from the soul will stimulate your "energetic senses" - causing you to pay attention even if at first you don't know why - or don't like the message. It will have a feeling of "right" about it even if your ego doesn't agree.
3. Communication from the soul will often have a quality of unusualness - be illogical, strangely coincidental, out of the ordinary, repetitious, weird, impossible or miraculous and sometimes even painful or uncomfortable, anything to make you take notice.
4. Communication from the soul is quiet, peaceful, loving, gentle and respectful. The soul will always respects your free will. Other messages are often characterized by impatience, anger, blame and guilt.
5. Communication from the soul will carry a feeling of great light, joy, enthusiasm and energy. The soul knows your true path is the one that gives you the most joy and aliveness. Other messages carry heavy emotional charges such as tension, anxiety, fear or uneasiness.
6. Communication from the soul usually incorporates both individual and greater good. (The soul always sees the bigger picture). Other messages exclude one or the other.
7. Communication from the soul possesses no time-line or sense of urgency, and is infinite-

ly patient and loving. Other messages often make you feel you must act immediately or all is lost, and carry an air of desperation.
8. Communication from the soul will persist and keep coming back over time. Other messages will fade rather quickly.
9. Actions and efforts based on information from the soul will go quickly and easily with much help, often with a lack of awareness of time passing. Efforts which are out of harmony with your soul and the universe will go badly, seem to drag on, take much longer than expected, and promote feelings of unhappiness, stress, conflict and/or boredom

37

Purpose vs. Passion

Those of us who believe we have a purpose in life are considered well blessed. Having a purpose gives us goals and direction, and provides value for our lives. It can be something we enjoy doing, are good at, or just something we think is worthwhile for others or for the world.

There was a time when I equated purpose with passion. But I have learned they are quite different.

Purpose is outer oriented and involved with other people and the physical world. Whether it's production of things or services, or the creation of widgets, or the solutions to problems, purpose is externally directed, rational, linear and quantitatively measured. We base our success on how many people are affected, how many customers served, how many clients seen, how many albums or books sold, or how many workshops sold out.

And most of the time we measure this success by how much money we make because of it. We derive our self-worth from these numbers, and if the numbers are high, we feel valued.

Often, we feel our purpose is even bestowed on us by some higher power and it is our destiny to fulfill that purpose in this lifetime. It gives us a sense of importance and belonging.

Passion, on the other hand, is inner oriented and self-directed. It is usually not based on rational choices or what others need or want. Passion comes from purely internal motivation even if no one else is interested, which is why those following their passion are often thought of as slightly irrational. Unlike purpose, passion comes from the soul.

Creating from passion is a multi-layered, multi-dimensional process – it often proceeds without a specific plan and is guided by intuition rather than reason.

What you are creating is valuable because it is your own self-expression, your own creation and you feel completed and whole while you are engaged in its creation or process. While you may be frustrated that large numbers of people don't value it as much as you do, you are nonetheless compelled to keep creating and keep looking for ways to share your creation with others.

Purpose is what satisfies most humans as they

navigate the physical world. But purpose is dependent on the outside world and as such is always precarious since it relies on external circumstances. This source of personal value can vanish at any time.

Passion is what brings joy and wonder, and often results in emerging genius.

Think of Van Gogh who sold hardly anything during his lifetime, or J. K. Rowling who was turned down by every major publisher of popular fiction. Passion is internal and survives even the most extreme external battering. In fact, passion can be the one source of joy and healing that keeps us balanced when our external world gets crazy.

In the last few years some of you may have noticed that what you had always thought of as your passion has left, often with nothing to replace it. You feel bereft and purposeless. You feel you have no value and have thus lost interest in life. This may be because, you, like me, have confused passion and purpose.

What you have lost, is purpose.

In my experience, this in-between time (although uncomfortable) is a necessary and important bridge between purpose and passion. This is a time when we are required to generate our own feelings of value and self-worth. Ultimately our value here on Earth is simply our own unique experience, and how that experience adds to the experience of all humans.

The life of a beggar on the street and the life of the highest paid CEO have the same value. It is important that I realize I don't have to DO anything to be valuable. Simply existing is enough. It may take some time, but the space in between losing purpose and discovering passion is a much needed bridge between external vs internal validation.

Once we have struggled with, and accepted for ourselves, this inner oriented validation, we are ready to find and fully unleash our passion. Passion comes from the sum total, the whole of our life experience, expressed in our own unique way, in whatever form intrigues us.

For me, my purpose and my passion turned out to be many of the same things. But since my creations are now inner directed, they no longer require effort. I can't wait to get to work even if I have no idea what I will create that day. My creations come easily and I love the process.

My passion directs my focus and my behavior. I never know whether any creation will be accepted or valued by others, but it doesn't matter. I am compelled to create in certain directions anyway. And when I am engaged in my passions, all time falls away and I am delighted by even the most mundane tasks necessary to bring them to fruition.

I had to be patient with myself. Self-validation

did not come easily. But now that I am creating with passion, I can't imagine living any other way.

Section Eight
The Aesthetic Imperative

38
Creative Expression

As we move into a state of closer contact with our souls, creativity becomes almost imperative. This is because the soul yearns for expression, and creativity is the means for that expression.

This yearning for expression can be a big problem for many of us today however, since our culture has an outdated and limited view of what creativity means.

Culturally, we have tended to think of a creative person as one who is engaged in the fine arts; someone who draws, paints, composes music or writes fiction or poetry. When encouraging people to engage in creative projects, I am always amazed by how often people say,

"Oh, I can't do that. I'm not creative".

They think they're not creative because they can't draw a straight line, stay on tune or compose a poem.

Our culture tends to confuse creativity with reproducing something that resembles some other thing that people call art. While reproducing a work similar to something someone else has done may help us gain some technical proficiency, it is not true creativity coming from the soul.

We also make the mistake of thinking that a creative person will exhibit creativity in everything they do. This is also a mistake. People recognized as creative in one area, may or may not be talented in another. Just because you can't draw or sing doesn't mean you are not creative.

Creativity is a process that expands far beyond what we usually call fine arts, and may only be evident in one medium.

Today, we are beginning to realize that innovation in technology, medicine, and even business is also creative. People like Steve Jobs and Bill Gates are nothing if not creative, even though their creations are not in art museums. (Although Steve Jobs' creations may one day be in museums, if they aren't already.)

Today we also recognize food as an artistic medium. Television shows like Top Chef have elevated what used to be simply a mechanism for survival into a fine art.

While gourmet cooking does not interest everyone, we all have to eat, so food creativity is available to us all. The plethora of cooking shows and recipes available on TV, the internet and Facebook attest to how many people are now exercising their creativity in this medium.

Most of us also don't realize how many ways creativity can manifest itself.

For some people it comes out in their ability to organize an office or a group of people. For others it has to do with how a person chooses their style of dress or home décor. Building a stone patio or deck, creating computer games, solving cyber security problems or counseling clients are all ways people exercise their creativity and express their passions.

Since all humans have souls, all people are creative.

But every soul is different and consequently every human is different. That means each human will create in a different way. The great artists and composers attained their greatness because they somehow found a way to allow the uniqueness that was all theirs to come out in their creations.

Creativity is the passionate expression of the soul.

Rather than strive to create things that look like what others do, our souls want us to create according to our own uniqueness. If your creation does not look like anyone else's, good for you. Even though we may find inspiration in others' creations, we often don't give ourselves credit for creating something that ultimately reflects our own unique being, rather than what inspired us in the first place.

The key to finding your creative passion is simply to do what you enjoy. Most of us don't realize that even great artists had to start somewhere, and often were not very good when they began. What counts is not what you create at the beginning, but whether you enjoy doing it.

From my experience working in many different media, I almost always start out creating what I would call "duds". But I have learned that if I enjoy the process, I will get better and better.

Many artistic media these days are greatly enhanced by knowing the many different tools and techniques available to work with. When you start out, you don't know these things. The more you learn, and the more you practice, the more satisfying the process and the product will become. If you enjoy the medium you are working in, keep going.

Exercising your creativity in whatever way is passionate for you, is also one of the most important ways you have to replenish your energy field. When we are tired, burned out or exhausted from all the energy draining experiences our lives may hold, creating is what brings us back, what replenishes our energy, and lights our fires.

When making hard choices about how to manage your time, the last thing to go should be what sparks your passion.

Loving yourself means allowing whatever time is needed to replenish your energy field. Be fearless and forge ahead. Take classes, find online tutorials. Today you can increase your knowledge of anything easily and inexpensively through the internet. Above all, don't compare your creations to others. Just enjoy the process.

39

May You Walk in Beauty

Why and how does a good piece of art affect us emotionally, mentally and spiritually?

I have always been deeply touched by the Navajo blessing, "May you walk in beauty". Beauty, for the Navajo, means more than simply the arrangement of a sand painting or the aesthetic quality of one's outer environment. It also includes the quality of one's relationships with oneself, as well as with one's fellow humans, with animals, and even with what we would call inorganic aspects of the environment.

For the Navajo, the word "beauty" expresses the benevolent and harmonious quality of all relationships.

Like the Navajo, I believe beauty is about relationships, and also about the meaning found within those relationships.

Meaning is significant connection.

The work of art makes significant connections within itself and with the outside world so that the observer or listener can relate meaningfully with it as well, thus expanding his or her awareness in a way that would have been impossible or unlikely otherwise.

Great works of art are human creations where the parts are purposefully arranged to support and enhance one another, but also where the whole that is the work of art connects meaningfully to things outside itself, thus becoming a part of larger systems within the greater culture.

For the Navajo, all of life is a work of art that always includes nature and humanity, both individually and as a group.

Truly great art contains meaning not just for the culture from which it originated, but for the entire human condition. The greater the number of relationships, the more complex they are, and the greater the engagement of the observer or listener, the more profound and beautiful the piece.

A good photograph, for example, isolates a portion of the physical world, thus causing us to become aware of the internal relationships of the elements in the photo in a way that may not have been possible if we had been looking at the scene without the frame.

The photographer is asking us to look at our surroundings in a new way, appreciating colors, relationships, juxtapositions, expressions, etc., that we could have missed otherwise. In other words, the work of art expands our consciousness with new meaning, whether that be appreciation for beauty not noticed before, humor, inspiration, insight, pathos, or sometimes even horror or disgust.

An artist creates environments where natural beauty can be more easily perceived and appreciated in new and different ways.

An artist also creates beauty where there was none before, making a beautiful sculpture from rusted car parts, an abstract painting on a blank canvas or an incredible wall hanging from old fabric scraps.

An artist can turn ugliness into grace, and junk into heirlooms.

An artist transforms our perceptions by pulling meaning out of thin air, then asking our consciousness to expand enough to take it in.

An artist sees beauty in everything.

An artist sees significance in harmony, but also in dissonance, in symmetry but also asymmetry, in light but also in dark, in perfection, but also in imperfection, as well as in the relationships between and among all of them.

An artist sees beauty where others may not have seen it before, and asks us to participate as well.

This participation, and the expanded consciousness that results from it, ultimately nudges us into considering ourselves as complex works of art as well.

Every human being is a masterpiece of meaningful relationships that is totally unique and like no other. But it often takes an artist to demonstrate this truth for each of us. It is our very imperfection that contributes to our greatest beauty. This is the difference between a handmade work of art and something made by machine. The mass-produced item can be flawless if truly well made, but it is not a work of art because it is flawless.

A great work of art is priceless because it is like no other.

It contains certain asymmetries and flaws, conflicts and oppositions, individual flourishes and special quirks, which give it a riveting interest that holds our attention like nothing else. It contains relationships and conjunctions, order and coherence, insights and connections, that help us appreciate and understand the world in a new way. It engages us emotionally, mentally and spiritually and expands both our consciousness and very being by its existence.

Each of us is also a priceless work of art because each of us is a complex set of relationships like no other. But because most of us are not yet aware of it, we still often see ourselves as old fabric scraps or rusted car parts that are practically worthless. And any worth we do perceive usually comes from what we do in the world, not what we are.

A work of art doesn't have to do anything.

Its relationships and connections generate meaning and worth by its mere presence. Like scraps of cloth and rusted car parts, those things we call problems, crises or imperfections in our lives are the very elements that form the core of the masterpiece. As we expand our consciousness to appreciate art, we draw ever closer to the unique and precious beauty of our own being.

For each of us is both a unique bundle of meaningful and complex relationships, and a consciousness that is capable of expanding and creating in new and profound ways.

As we come to appreciate the masterpiece of our own being, we awaken the artist/creator at the core of our own individuality, who longs for expression.

And then we finally recognize ourselves as both a work of art and the artist who created it. Perhaps the true mystery of art lies in how much we are all integrally a part of that mystery.

40

Lessons of Physical Creation

So many of the important lessons in my life have come from time spent in the creation of physical objects. First it was painting and drawing, and then jewelry and stained glass. Now I work in fiber and photography. I have always loved writing.

Many of these lessons were easier to learn because the creation was simply a fun project and its success or failure was of no importance. But even when I worked as a full-time professional stained glass artisan, life lessons were always presenting themselves.

The first thing I learned in stained glass was that even when you have a deadline and a client breathing down your neck, you cannot work with glass when you're irritated or having a bad day.

You cut glass by etching a line on the glass with a cutter, then breaking the glass along the line. If the break doesn't go as planned, it can be very dangerous, as in the glass shattering in your hands or shards going through your leg or foot.

Cutting glass takes focus and precision. I quickly found that irritability rattled my energy field, influencing my ability to focus, and even disturbed my physical coordination so that cutting precisely was difficult.

The more mistakes, the worse the irritability, until I finally realized what a perilous situation I was creating. A few small injuries taught me how easy it would be to lose a finger or cut an artery as a result of a bad mood. I learned that when irritable it was better to walk away than risk almost certain injury and/or a ruinous mistake.

From these experiences, I discovered how negative emotions influence everything I do and every interaction I have. My irritability, anger or frustration spreads friction, casts a dark cloud on all my efforts, and ensures that things will not go as well as they could.

Stained glass also taught me how mistakes can be blessings in disguise.

When you work at a glass studio you have access to one-of-a-kind pieces of art glass that can never be reproduced. If I made a mistake and cut one of these the wrong way, or it broke differently than I planned, my piece was ruined.

Unless I could see it in a new way.

If I could somehow work the break line into the design in a different way that complemented and enhanced the project, the piece often turned out even better than I had originally planned. The necessity of saving the glass, and the piece, forced me to dig deep and find creativity I didn't even know I had.

Now I work in fiber. I make quilts, wall hangings and quilted bags. I allow the fabric to determine the design and thus the kind of construction needed for the project. But this means that I almost never use patterns, and have to come up with new and different construction techniques all the time. I make many mistakes, but the mistakes teach me new ways of doing things.

From working with fiber I have learned not to be afraid of even the most ambitious or seemingly impossible (for me) projects.

I just take things one step at a time, and before long, the project is finished and is usually much better than I imagined. I have learned that mistakes are part of the process and do not berate myself for them. Instead I use them as ways to push my creativity and improve my technique.

Creating tangible objects not only allows my soul a way to express itself, but the physical nature of the creation process offers analogies and metaphors for the rest of life, and makes it easier to accept and learn from mistakes, failures and disappointments.

Beverly Crane, PhD.

It has also given me the courage and confidence to start projects I haven't the faintest idea how to do, and has provided the patience and perseverance needed to see them through to the end.

It has also taught me that we can use our creative ability in every aspect of physical life, from cooking and gardening, to home repair, carpentry, building stonewalls, and just plain doodling.

When we bring creativity into our everyday lives, we find it can be indispensable not only for solving problems, but in how we look at problems. Because of the lessons of physical creativity, I no longer worry when faced with a problem I don't know how to solve. I know I will manifest the solution eventually, if I just keep at it.

41
Limitation and Creativity

One of the most vexing parts of living in physical reality is the fact that resources seem limited. If what you see is what you get, then reality is already created and there is only so much of it.

In a traditional worldview where energy reality is unperceived and the only reality is physical, there is only so much of everything. This means that if you have more, then I have less, and vice versa. Unless we are incredibly wealthy, we are constantly bemoaning our lack of abundance.

As a result of this perception of limited resources, we have created a culture where competition is not only the norm, but the approved and exalted way of providing food for our tables and roofs over our heads. And all too often, this competitive drive results in a cutthroat kind of capitalism where many are hurt so a few can gain.

While it is easy to deplore this state of affairs and wish, and even strive for, a more equitable way of distributing resources, we should also keep in mind that limitation has its value.

Limitation is almost always the underlying ground of creativity and a necessary prod for expanding our potential.

Just think about the times you've been at your most creative.

For me, it has almost always been when I have lacked something I needed. As a very abundance-challenged graduate student, I found that buying discounted vegetables and making a huge pot of soup on Sunday would give me more than enough good food for the week ahead.

Whether it was making a fish hook from a paperclip or fashioning a bookcase from three baskets turned on their sides and fastened to the wall, my creativity was able to turn lack into abundance at the very least, and great design and aesthetic pleasure at the most.

I have to admit, I had a great teacher in a foster grandparent on whose farm I worked in the summer as a teenager.

Whenever anything broke or needed to be replaced, rather than go into town to buy something new, my grandfather simply rummaged around the farm, picking up this and that, and before long, the problem was solved.

This creativity was exercised not only on simple necessities like plumbing and construction, but his more complex hobbies that included a Model T and a small private plane. Through watching him, I came to understand that limitation often leads to the most ingenious solutions and discoveries.

If it weren't for lack or limitation, or running down a blind alley, we would not be forced to find new ways of doing things, to explore unfamiliar avenues and/or try new flavors. If you are hungry, lots of things taste good that might not have tasted good before.

When confronted by necessity, we are pushed beyond our comfort limits, forced out of the boxes we have made for ourselves, and exposed to vistas not available to us previously.

This principle can be seen especially well in the arts. The painter's challenge is the fact that his canvas only has two dimensions. How can he create a three dimensional-like image with this limitation?

In fact, artists often give themselves limitations just to make their work more interesting and creative.

I know a quilter who purposely uses only saved

scraps of cloth from other projects just like her grandmother, even though she could easily buy whatever kind, and however much material she wanted. For her, the process of quilt making is much more creative because she has limited herself in this way.

I also know of an African artist who limits himself to working solely with caps and metal neck rings from bottles. From these cast-off items he creates three dimensional, woven fabric-like sculptures of breathtaking beauty, that cover entire walls. The creativity in his art forms is truly amazing because the items he creates with are not only common trash, but limited to only two small shapes.

If you're an artist (and everybody is), limitation can actually be fun.

Even if you don't think you're an artist, when it seems like you're at the end of the road, it's very helpful to realize the important role of lack and limitation in getting us to expand and actualize our potentials. Limitation forces us to move beyond what we think is possible.

Could this be one of the major purposes of physical reality?

Section Nine
Energy and Your Body

42
Synergy and Health

"Synergy" is a word used to describe the synchronized energy created by a group working harmoniously toward a common goal that produces a combined effect greater than the sum of the parts. This word can also be used to describe the synchronized energy among cells working together to create health in the human body.

We have long thought that there is little conscious control over the physical body.

From quantum physics however, we now know that consciousness does affect energy. This means that creating synergy in our physical bodies can be accomplished by our conscious intention, and that the condition of energy relationships in our bodies can impact our physical well being.

All the cells in our bodies, as well as our DNA, have energy fields around them. When these fields overlap, they share information. This is how our DNA communicates instructions so that the cells know what they're supposed to do.

When all cells are working together harmoniously toward the greater good of the whole body, we enjoy perfect health.

I call this kind of energy "quantum synergy" because it is synergy operating on a subatomic level in living things, and can be viewed as the equivalent of "quantum entanglement" in the inorganic field of quantum physics. Quantum entanglement is the energetic principle that connects all things on a subatomic level.

But "entanglement" is an unfortunate choice of words when trying to understand how energetic behavior creates health and well-being in living things

Although we may have many energy "entanglements" in our bodies and in our lives, our goal should be to consciously unravel these entanglements and replace them with synergistically harmonious energetic relationships, whether between the cells in our body or in our relationships with friends and family.

If synergy among cells describes complete health, disease and physical discomfort must come from a breakdown of harmony somewhere in the system.

Why would this happen?

The body is also a part of the soul, which is in constant communication with the cells and DNA. This makes the body a part of the soul's communication system.

When your actions, attitude, or beliefs become misaligned with your greater good, that misalignment often shows up in your body in the form of disease or discomfort. The good news is that the symptoms and/or areas of discomfort are also part of the soul's communication system and are designed to give you clues as to where the misalignment may be occurring.

When I was in graduate school, I was often sick with colds or flu, so I asked myself what these symptoms might be trying to tell me.

I noticed that when I had a cold, my senses shut down. I couldn't smell or taste, my eyes were watery, blurring my vision, and my sinuses inflamed so that my hearing was not as good as usual.

Since our physical senses take in information from our environment, I wondered if my body was trying to tell me that I was on information overload, and needed to shut down and take a break from my hectic schedule.

I decided to conduct an experiment.

At that time, I was not married and had no children, thus no real responsibilities other than to myself. So whenever I felt that prodromal period when I knew a cold was coming on, I retreated to my room, shut the door, and declared a mental health day. I'd take a warm bath, relax on my bed, nap and read novels or magazines for a whole day.

And guess what? The next day I'd feel great, and the cold never materialized.

I continued to follow this ritual with great results until I got married and had children. When my kids were young and I could no longer indulge in this kind of behavior, I was sick often. Now that they're grown and on their own, I can once again take care of myself, and, as long as I do, I rarely get colds.

Cancer is another disease that is fairly straightforward when viewed metaphorically. In cancer the quantum synergy of the body breaks down to such an extent that groups of cells disregard the good of the whole and go off on their own.

Usually the kind of cancer and its location in the body will give clues as to what the problem may be. When I had cancer, it disfigured my face and jaw, and thus my ability to speak and appear in public. It was trying to tell me I needed to leave my job in academia and search out a new profession.

Once we become more accustomed to our souls' little pokes and prods, that is, those niggling feelings that something's not going well or doesn't feel right, it's not as necessary for the soul to speak through the body in such a dramatic way.

Pain and disease are the communications of last resort because they always get our attention.

When we are busy and/or under lots of stress, we don't have time to tune into our body or feel into our energy field. Stress itself is an energy full of friction and conflict because it usually has to do with trying to meet someone else's expectations, or because we have conflicting expectations of ourselves. When you feel into the energy of stress, you can understand how easily it can disrupt the natural energy flow of your body.

The best way to assess the quantum synergy (or its absence) in your physical body is to feel into it every day.

Giving yourself quiet time, engaging in meditation, yoga, conscious breathing and exercise have long been touted as healthy practices, but understanding the necessity of harmonious energy relationships in your body and the role you have in promoting them, underscores how much your conscious choices affect your health.

What does quantum synergy feel like? It feels like a C chord played by a full orchestra. It feels like a walk in a maple woods on a bright fall day. It feels like a hot shower after a hard workout. You'll know it when you're there. So take time for yourself and FEEL.

43

Body Intelligence

The phrase "body intelligence" seems like an oxymoron. We think of intelligence as active consciousness coming from the mind, with the body being the passive victim of influences like viruses, toxins and bacteria, over which we have no control.

About 20 years ago the new science of psychoneuroimmunology suggested that emotions and the unconscious could affect the immune system and thus our state of health or disease. But this connection still was far from the intelligent control that we associate with the mind.

It may therefore be quite surprising to think of the body as an active intelligence that is separate from, but no less important than the mind.

The human body does indeed have two intelligence systems. The first is the one we are all familiar with; the brain and central nervous system, which also includes the emotions. The second is the body itself.

The reason we have never thought of the body as intelligent is because it doesn't seem to respond to our attempt to control it with our minds. We would dearly love to be able to protect ourselves from getting diseases, and to heal ourselves quickly if we should experience illness or accidents. But that doesn't happen.

If the body is intelligent, it definitely has a mind of its own.

This is because the mental intelligence system and the bodily intelligence system have two different agendas and operate according to two different sets of rules.

The brain and central nervous system, with help from the emotions, are programed to keep the physical body on Earth for as long as possible. As new beings on Earth (babies), we create a specific energy pattern called the ego to help with this task. The purpose of the ego and mental intelligence is to protect us and control our environment as much as possible in order to make sure we are safe and get our needs met.

The mind does this by receiving pain or pleasure signals from the body and the emotions, and recording the circumstances in memory so that we will know to avoid or repeat these experiences in the future. In this way we can control our environment to the best of our ability.

Body intelligence, rather than being aligned with the ego, is instead aligned with the soul. As such, it has a completely different agenda than mental intelligence.

The purpose of this body/soul alliance is not physical well being, but spiritual well being. Consequently, the body is programmed to cease to exist at some point because spiritual well being depends on accumulated wisdom from as many different experiences as possible.

Shedding our body and then acquiring another in different times, spaces and/or dimensions allows us to grow our wisdom and understanding, and so increase our spiritual consciousness.

Our state of health and disease is also a function of the body's alignment with the soul. Physical symptoms and/or disease can hold clues to imbalances in our relationship with the world, and/or offer us gifts we could not get any other way. For example, Diabetes can urge us to reassess our relationship to the sweet things in life, while a cold or flu offers us time and space to rest that we might not have felt entitled to take otherwise.

Body intelligence not only has a different agenda, but also operates by a different set of rules. Mental intelligence is logical and operates in a linear fashion. It follows logic and the Newtonian laws of physics that govern physical matter. Body intelligence follows energetic or quantum laws.

Like the soul, the body is always trying to communicate. But like other kinds of energetic communication, we usually don't recognize its communication because it is the opposite of the verbal, linear, logical kind of language we normally use.

Communication from the body is multi layered, symbolic and multidimensional. It comes in symbolic images, experiences and whole insights, often in complete gestalts with no linear sequence. It can also be conveyed on certain energetic vibrations and frequencies.

The next chapter explores some of these communication channels.

44

The Language of the Body

The body tries to communicate with us in two very specific ways. The first and most subtle is through certain energetic signals that clue us into positive or negative situations or choices that we may be facing.

Take, for example, telling a lie. Most of us try not to deceive, but we've all done it. Think for a moment about how it feels to tell a lie. Imagine standing in front of someone you know well and telling a fib. Then you realize they know you are telling a lie.

Notice how you feel.

Observe how your body reacts.

You will probably feel some negative feeling, vibration or frequency somewhere in your body that may actually feel physical. You may feel like you swallowed a stone, or that you're going to lose your lunch. You could have a sinking feeling in your stomach or a catch in your throat.

Carefully take note of whatever feeling this is for you, and then watch for it again in the future. Your body will give you the same energetic signal when you make a choice that is not in your best spiritual interest, or when you turn in a direction that is less than optimal for you.

Our bodies gives us these signals all the time, but usually we ignore them because they're subtle, have no physical cause, and our actions at the time seem to be emotionally or logically justified. But remember, body communication is not logical, nor is it a function of the pleasure/pain dualism of the emotions. It is important to pay attention nonetheless.

Now imagine being in a place where you feel loved and safe, and excited about what life has to offer. Keep working with your imagination to create a place and a feeling of perfect trust and well being.

When you have achieved this goal, feel your body respond energetically to this fantasy. Feel how your vibration rises and all frequencies are perfectly in sync. You feel in complete harmony with yourself and everything around you. Pay attention to this feeling for your body will repeat it when you are on the right path, and/or when you have made a choice that is just right for you.

I call these subtle energetic signals "body energetics". Once you have mastered these body communications you will have also established a direct link to your soul, and can benefit from this information in every choice or decision you face.

Body energetics is a skill that will also help in your physical well being because these subtle signals come into play before we develop full-blown symptoms of disease.

If we heed these signals correctly, we can often (but not always) prevent both minor and major illnesses from coming our way.

Physical symptoms are the second way our bodies communicate with us. If we have not been cognizant of the body energetics that alert us to our interaction with ourselves and the world, then we may experience full-blown symptoms and physical disease.

But even in this case, our bodies continue to speak to us. The location of the symptom, the kind of pain and the specific disability or pain caused by the symptom are sources of information about the imbalance we are experiencing.

For example, colds shut down our senses so we are forced to take a vacation from the world, even if we choose to try to work or perform everyday tasks while sick. All of us have experienced trying to work with a cold; the feeling of going through our daily routine like a zombie, unable to interact with others or our environment in anything other than a most superficial way.

Flu is a more severe reminder of the need to rest

and take a break. The flu knocks us out completely, forcing us to take to our beds and do nothing but rest.

Each part of our body has symbolic meaning that calls out to us to be understood.

Stomach problems have to do with digestion, taking in something that disagrees or poisons us. If you have stomach problems, ask yourself what you have encountered lately that you are having trouble assimilating or integrating into your life.

Do you often have sore throats? A sore throat literally speaks to us of words left unsaid, of self-expression stymied or squashed. What do you need to say, and to whom?

So many of us suffer from back pain. Our back bones and muscles hold us up straight and allow us to move freely. Back pain often signifies a lack of confidence and self-love that keeps us from standing up for ourselves in the face of others who might not approve.

Physical symptoms are information. But this communication is symbolic in form. Until we learn the language of symbolism, we will miss the cues.

There are many good books on learning the symbolism of body communication, (*Your Body Speaks Your Mind* by Deb Shapiro and *The Secret Language of Your Body* by Inna Segal, for example). These books can point you in the right direction in terms of deciphering the information physical symptoms present.

But remember that body communication is intensely personal. One size does not fit all. You will have to feel into the energy of your particular symptom and the meaning it may have for you. You may find clues in a book. You can ask for additional information in meditation, dreams or synchronicities, or you may have to just feel into the energy for a correct interpretation.

Serious and/or life threatening illnesses present a more life changing spiritual challenge. When confronted with a potentially terminal disease, we are being given notice of an impending spiritual transformation.

We can transform from a physical being into a purely energetic one (death), or we can use this experience to radically transform our lives.

If you study the stories of those who have had seemingly miraculous recoveries, you will notice that life after the disease is not in any way the same as before. We are being presented with an opportunity to experience life in a new way that often entails entirely new belief systems, attitudes, environments and appreciation for life.

Once we begin to understand how body intelligence works, we realize that we don't have to think of our body and mind as operating independently of one another.

Despite having different agendas and different sets of rules, these two intelligent parts of our being can work together. Paying attention to the body's efforts to reach us will greatly enhance both our physical and spiritual well being.

Communication is a two-way street. In the next few chapters I will address two-way communication; how to let the body know how it can cooperate with our minds, and how to gain information directly from body intelligence.

In two-way communication we can establish a truly collaborative effort in maximizing our physical and spiritual well being.

Deb Shapiro, Your Body Speaks Your Mind.
Inna Segal, The Secret Language of Your Body.

45

Visualization and Healing

Back in the early 1980s, I came across a book that would change my life.

The book was called *Getting Well Again* by Carl and Stephanie Simonton. He was an oncologist and she a psychologist. Together they discovered a promising way to help cancer patients heal their disease. They found that when cancer patients visualized their immune systems fighting cancer cells, the cancer diminished or disappeared completely.

Back then, the video game Pac-Man was a big hit, and the Simontons used this game's notoriety to demonstrate their technique. Pac-Men were little round bubbles with huge mouths that gobbled up everything in their path.

The Simontons suggested that patients imagine

It's All About Energy: Adventures in Expanded Reality

their white blood cells were Pac-men and that these voracious allies could be directed to wherever the cancer might be in order to gobble up those unhealthy cells.

Because this method seemed so off-the-wall at the time, Carl's fellow oncologists were reluctant to send patients to the Simonton's clinic. Consequently, most of their patients were those that all other oncologists had given up on. The success of this methodology was therefore all the more surprising.

After this book came out, there followed others that touted visualization and imagery as important tools for healing. The radical nature of this approach however, prevented researchers from investigating it, and doctors from taking it seriously. As a result, this methodology fell by the wayside and was soon forgotten by most people.

But I never forgot.

I decided that if visualization could cure cancer, it could cure other things as well. In the years since I discovered this book, I have used this technique over and over with myself, family, friends and clients, and found it to be very effective.

My first success came when I was able to cure a persistent urinary tract infection that had sent me to the emergency room over and over again. The last time I had a UT infection was over 30 years ago when I was on an overnight car trip from Wisconsin to Texas.

In the middle of the night, in the middle of nowhere, far from any known hospital, I got a UT infection. With no emergency room available, I had no choice but to try the Simonton's method. After a couple of intensive hours of visualization, both the pain and the infection were gone. AND IT DIDN'T CAME BACK, EVER!

When my son was six, he got a staph infection on the back of his hand. The doctor prescribed a very expensive antibiotic, probably because staph is so serious. Since the infection was on his hand where I could closely monitor it, I decided to try visualization first.

My son was obsessed with school busses at the time, so I told him to imagine hoards of school busses traveling around his body picking up white blood cells and transporting them to his hand, where they spilled out of the busses and attacked the infection. Additional busses brought more fighters, and took away the tired ones to rest and fight again.

Within a few hours I could see definite improvement, so we just continued with the visualization. The infection was gone in a couple of days with no antibiotic needed. It didn't come back either.

Recently a close family member used visualization to successfully turn around his terminal illness after doctors had given up.

Visualization is amazing but it's not magic or a miracle. It's communicating with the body through energetic means, and it's something you can do for yourself.

The advantages are many. It is not invasive, has no negative side effects, and can often encourage healing in other parts of your body as well. In many cases, it seems to be permanent, with much less chance of relapse.

The disadvantages, if you can call them that, are that visualization takes honesty, curiosity, creativity, commitment and dedication on your part. It is not a pill you can swallow and forget about. This dedication, however, may be what convinces your body that you are really committed to continuing your life on Earth and creating a healthier you, resulting not just in the elimination of the disease you are targeting, but general improvement of overall well-being.

The only other disadvantage is that you may have to confront a medical team that thinks you're crazy despite your improvement.

If you would like to try this technique yourself, here are some guidelines.

1. Before starting a visualization routine, be sure and remove any external factors or internal blocks that might prevent the body from responding.

    External factors could be environmental toxins or allergens, drug side effects, drug interactions, or foreign objects. Internal blocks may be stuck emotions left over from past trauma where the emotion was not allowed to diffuse itself and now needs to be released.

There may also be subconscious reasons why being sick is serving you.

2. Visualization is best done in a calm, relaxed state much like meditation or guided imagery. While it is often easier to have someone else guiding your visualization, it is not necessary. You can easily create and conduct a successful visualization routine on your own.

3. While it is important to know the nature of the disease and how it is disturbing the healthy functioning of the body, it is not necessary to conform your visualization to strict anatomical or functional details. In fact, visualization works best when it is more symbolic than literal, for example, Pac-men or school busses.

4. It is important to engage as many of your senses as possible in your visualization. If you are visualizing Pac-men battling cancer cells, the more vividly you can see, hear, smell, taste and feel the battle, the more effective your visualization will be. The more actively you participate, the more your body takes you seriously.

5. If you are a pacifist and fighting Pac-men turn you off, don't worry. You can always design a more compassionate way to deal with the situation. You could imagine golden fairy dust surrounding the cancer cells, dissolving them or turning them into healthy tissue.

6. You can also talk out loud to your body. This method is particularly effective for people who are not visual. Talking out loud provides much more resonance and energy than just internal thought. Talk to your body just as you would a friend. Thank if for all it has done for you, and then give it detailed instructions on how it can serve you.

Your body wants a relationship with you. Pay attention to what it is trying to tell you and use the information wisely.

O. Carl Simonton, Stephanie Matthews-Simonton and James L. Creighton, Getting Well Again (Reprinted 1992)

46

The Role of the Emotions

Even though Body Intelligence and Mental Intelligence are best understood as two separate systems, they are indelibly connected by the emotions.

Think of emotions as energy in motion, or e-motion. Emotions either propel you toward something pleasurable or beneficial, or repel you away from things that are painful and dangerous. Emotions by their very nature are meant to flow.

Since emotions are energetic, they travel through the energy meridians that make up the body's energy system. Although emotions are specifically designed to respond to physical events and situations, they flow through, and are released from the energy system, usually without permanently affecting the physical body.

When you experience an emotion, let's say fear, it gives you information you can (hopefully) act upon.

You see a snake in your path and your heart leaps to your throat in fear. You stop, and slowly back up. You watch as the snake slithers leisurely away into the grass. Then you breathe a sigh of relief and continue on your way.

In this case, the fear has been felt, acted upon, and then released when the danger is passed. The emotion has done its job, passed through the meridians and is then dismissed.

The problems come when emotions don't get released. Then they become stuck in the meridians causing emotional anguish, and often even physical pain and disease.

In childhood trauma when a parent is involved, the child is often not able to protect or remove him/herself from the danger. In this case, fear, and all the other negative emotions that surround the situation get tucked away in the meridians. The situation may be so painful and uncontrollable that these emotions become repressed and remain trapped even after the child grows up and is better able to manage his/her environment.

Belief systems are another cause of stuck emotions. If we have been taught that certain emotions are bad and should not be expressed, like anger, envy, jealousy, rage, disgust, etc., then we tend to repress these feelings, since to admit to them would mean having to confront a part of ourselves we deem as "bad".

Any time an emotion is not able to function in the way it was designed, that emotion is in danger of being repressed and trapped.

If we experience fear, but can't save ourselves from harm, if we experience anger, but can't express it because it's too dangerous, if we experience lust but think sex is bad, we will probably repress these feelings.

Grief is another emotion that often gets stuck because we never have control over when a loved one dies. Men, especially feel obligated to be strong for others who are openly grieving. Ironically, those that openly grieve will often be more emotionally healthy that those who stuff their feelings in an effort to serve others.

Trapped emotions are uncomfortable, and even unhealthy if they remain stuck long enough. Body Intelligence alerts us to this condition by strange emotional reactions to things that others have no problem with.

We may even experience unusual pains and physical discomfort that have no physical origins. Even when stuck emotions don't cause physical pain, they are most often the root of psychological issues like phobias, PTSD, relationship issues and other inappropriate and unconscious reactions and behaviors.

In the last few decades a new therapeutic modality has emerged to deal with trapped emotions.

Called Energy Psychology, it uses intention and meridian manipulation such as tapping, magnetics or rapid eye movement, to bring a trapped emotion to consciousness and physically release it.

The success of this methodology is demonstrated by the proliferation of these modalities and the plethora of practitioners who are now devoted to each of them. There are now so many of these therapies that it would be hard to identify all of them. However, some of the more well known are Emotional Freedom Technique (EFT), Thought Field Therapy (TFT), Neural Emotional Tapping (NET), EMDR, the Emotion Code, and WHEE.

Most tapping techniques seek to loosen and release stuck energy by identifying the meridian that corresponds to the issue or pain, and then tapping on a pressure point linked to that meridian until relief is felt.

While it is possible to learn all the meridians and corresponding psychological and physical symptoms, it is easier for most people to find a skilled practitioner rather than tackling what may seem like a huge learning curve.

There are two techniques, however, The Emotion Code developed by Dr. Bradley Nelsen and WHEE (Whole Health Easily and Efficiently) developed by

Daniel Benor, that have simplified their processes so that each can be easily mastered by a lay person. Their books are referenced at the end of the chapter.

Although single emotions can be successfully handled this way, there are situations that involve a number of emotions that form a constellation of interdependent energy relationships that feed off one another. Physical, sexual, emotional or energetic abuse of long standing, war, and abuse of self in the form of perfectionism, can all cause this negative energy feedback loop to form.

Although anger may be the primary emotion, other emotions such as hopelessness, despair, bitterness, resentment, etc. may also be part of the equation. These secondary emotions can vary greatly depending on the situation. If these emotions are not all identified, made conscious and released, the result is often chronic emotional or physical pain that is resistant to conventional treatment, and/or pops up again in a different part of the body after successful treatment in the first location.

This is why chronic pain seems so stubborn and unreceptive to many traditional treatments. Pain is the body's way of getting our attention so that the soul's work can be done.

Trapped emotions that are not released during one lifetime can and do follow a person into their next lifetime. Trapped emotions from a past life are even harder to recognize and release than from a current life, so it is important to deal with them now.

This is why chronic pain often (but not always) occurs as people get older. The longer the emotion remains stuck, and the closer we get to death, the more important it is to release it. Unfortunately, chronic pain is usually attributed to the aging process, so very few people understand its true origins and are able to get permanent relief.

There are a few medical doctors who do understand the link between chronic pain and the emotions. Dr. John E. Sarno started treating chronic pain decades ago by asking patients to focus on unconscious rage they may be hiding from themselves.

Rage is not a single emotion but usually consists of a constellation of emotions. His approach uses group work and individual psychotherapy to identify and release these emotions. With a success rate of 75%-88%, his work has now attracted many other doctors around the country who are practicing his method.

This network can be accessed on the internet by searching his name. He has also written a number of books that explain his approach. Although he does not use tapping techniques to release emotions, tapping would probably be of great benefit.

One of the things that almost all of these techniques have in common is that you don't have to fully re-experience traumatic emotions in order to release them (whew!). Just bringing these emotions to consciousness, understanding why they became stuck, and forgiving yourself for having them greatly facilitates release.

A statement of conscious intention to release is also important. Sometimes our issues and pains are bringing us certain advantages such as extra attention from friends and family and/or permission to avoid tasks and responsibilities we find burdensome. For complete emotional release, the body needs to know that you are ready to forego whatever these advantages might be. Tapping or other kinds of meridian manipulation completes the loosening process and sends the emotion gently on its way.

The good news is that recovering these buried emotions does not have to be traumatic or painful, and there are many techniques and practitioners available. Body intelligence reminds us that emotional harmony is an important part of physical well-being.

Books referenced:
Nelsen, Bradley, The Emotion Code
Benor, Daniel, Seven Minutes to Natural Pain Relief
Sarno, John E. The Divided Mind
_____Healing Back Pain

47
Dialoguing With the Body

We can start working in cooperation with the body by paying attention to how the body speaks to us, by communicating with the body through visualization, and by paying attention to the role of emotions. Ultimately, however, it would help greatly if we could actually ask our bodies questions and get answers back.

There is a way to do this.

The methodology behind this process is based on the Body Energetics system I discussed in the chapter on Body Intelligence. The condition of energy in your body, that is, the nature of its frequency and vibration, is affected by your interaction with your environment.

If a statement you make is true, or the answer to a question is positive, then your energy will reflect the positive energy generated by increasing its coherency, harmony and coordination among all systems.

When the situation, choice or question is negative, then your energy changes. It becomes more disjointed, uncoordinated and out of harmony with itself. These subtle differences can be felt if we pay attention. But they also register in our muscles in ways that can be tested and measured. Testing our muscles for strength or weakness can therefore give us information in a yes/no form.

Applied Kinesiology has developed a number of ways to test muscle strength or weakness. These methods can be adapted to enable mind-body dialogue.

The standard muscle test involves a skilled practitioner and a client. The client holds an arm out perpendicular to the body and then resists the practitioner's attempt to push the outstretched arm towards the floor. After a practice test to establish baseline strength, a yes/no question can be asked and then force applied.

If the muscles are strong, the answer is yes, if the answer is no, the muscles are weak and the practitioner is easily able to break any resistance.

The disadvantage of this method is that there always needs to be two people, and the one doing the testing needs to be skilled. However, there are many ways to practice muscle testing alone if you are willing to take the time to become skilled yourself.

One method is called the "sway test".

You stand straight with your knees unlocked and ask your body a yes or no question that you know the answer to. Observe your body, and whether or not it tends to sway forward or backward.

Usually a positive answer will cause the body to sway forward and a negative answer will cause the body to sway backward, but this is not always the case. Test yourself to make sure. You can test by saying "My name is (real name)", and then observe the direction of the sway. Then say, "My name is (false name), and observe.

You can also fill a milk jug with water and place it on a counter or shelf at shoulder height, ask your body a question and then try to lift the container. Although it will take practice, eventually you will be able to sense the difference in how easily you can lift the jug.

Another method uses the thumb and little finger of both hands. Make a circle with your thumb and little finger of one hand, then insert the thumb and little finger of your other hand into the circle you have just made and make a circle with these fingers forming two links. The ease at which you can pull your fingers apart will indicate yes or no answers.

Not everyone will have success with all of these methods. I cannot use the finger method, nor the jug method, but the sway test works well. Other people find the opposite is true.

Many people have difficulty using any of these methods because most of us are loath to give up control.

When we ask a question we usually want a specific answer and are afraid we will get the opposite. Fear of loss of control, and confronting uncomfortable truths will freeze us up and make any dialogue impossible. Fear of not being able to do it will also freeze us and therefore separate from the body.

However, for these reasons, a dowsing rod or pendulum may be a better choice. While emotions and desire of outcome can influence rods and pendulums as well, it seems easier to limit their influence because they are instruments.

Dowsing rods and pendulums also respond to the subtle changes in our muscles. They register those changes on the instrument by reversing the direction of movement. You can practice with a rod or pendulum simply by asking it to give you a "yes", and watching the direction of the swing, and then asking for a "no", and observing the change.

If you don't have a rod or pendulum and would like to try this method before buying anything, you can make a dowsing rod from a metal coat hanger.

Grasp the long part of the coat hanger loosely

in your fist. The metal is so thin that a loose grasp will easily allow the coat hanger to swing in both directions. Point the coat hanger straight ahead of you, and ask your question or state your name. If your grip is loose enough, you will notice the curled end of the coat-hanger moving to the right or left.

Whatever method you use will take time and patience to perfect. Body Energetics are subtle and it takes time and practice to gain confidence.

You can use this technique in many practical ways. The easiest way to begin is to ask your body about drug doses or food allergies. Remember all your questions must be yes/no questions.

Some suggestions:

Ask your body if a certain drug would have a beneficial effect on a physical problem.

Ask whether certain foods like coffee, sugar or alcohol are causing or exacerbating illness.

Ask if additional exercise would lower your blood pressure.

After you acquire a certain amount of confidence, you will find that using yes/no questions can enhance your intuitive abilities.

When you get yes/no answers that don't seem to make sense or don't deliver enough information, your intuition will begin to click in. You will automatically ask yourself, "Why doesn't this make sense? What else could be going on?" Then your intuition will give you an answer, sometimes a very surprising one. You can check the correctness of this intuitive hit by asking another yes/no question, that is, whether the intuitive hit is correct.

It's all very magical.

Section Ten
Some Practical Applications

48
Garden Magic

Living in expanded reality means being able to open your heart to connect energetically with everything around you.

Coming from our hearts with gratitude and appreciation opens lines of communication (via a quantum connection) that embraces us all. This connection not only gives us a profound sense of the sacredness of all creation, but can also provide many benefits

Take the garden, for example.

For many gardeners, weeding is one of the most frustrating chores, especially when the roots are deep, and /or the soil is dry, and all your efforts only produce weeds broken off at the top with roots still left to spring up yet again a short time later. How discouraging!

If this sounds familiar to you, try opening your heart and connecting to the weed energy in deep appreciation. Weeds are plants, and all plants are beautiful in their own way. We dislike weeds not because they are inherently ugly, but because they are growing where we don't want them. And as human creators, we do have the right to create gardens of our own design.

Let the weeds know that you truly appreciate them for their beauty, their tenacity, and their ability to fill the woods, meadows and roadsides with luscious green and dashes of color. Then lovingly explain that as much as you appreciate them, you have reserved this space for specific plants, and would appreciate their help in making room for those plants you've chosen.

Picture yourself easily disengaging the weeds and send that image to them so they know what you want them to do. Then grasp the weed and pull gently asking that it release itself, roots and all. You will be amazed at the difference!

You can also use this method with any four or six legged creatures that are feasting on your garden.

Sit in meditation, open your heart and connect with the kind of animal or insect that is causing the problem. Although you can ask them to leave completely if necessary, I usually offer to share.

For example, I offer one of four eggplants to the potato bugs if they will leave me the other three. I ask the deer to refrain from nipping off the bean buds after they have helped themselves the first time. I picture them doing what I ask and send that image out to them. Animals and insects have to eat too, but I find they seem to appreciate my willingness to share, and are eager to cooperate if I ask with an open heart.

If you have a small garden or only ornamental plants, you may not wish to share, and that's OK too. The key is to connect with an open and loving heart rather than seeing them as enemies to be conquered or vanquished. Force doesn't work in the energy dimension. Love and co-creation do.

49

Working With Nature Spirits

In 2014, I had the good fortune to spend two weeks in Iceland, a majestic country full of surprises and subtleties. One of the surprises I found there is that despite being the most educated and literate of all developed nations, most Icelanders believe in Elves.

Many Icelanders have their own personal stories about their encounters with these nature spirits, and even large earth moving projects are not undertaken without consideration of Elfin sensibilities. The government also acknowledges the existence of Elves and makes allowances for their needs when planning construction.

Our guide told us a story of one of his own encounters with Elves.

He and some friends had gone into the mountains to hunt geese, and made camp at the base of a magnificent cliff face. Without really thinking, they used the cliff for target practice and the ravine underneath for a latrine.

Suddenly everything that could go wrong, did go wrong. The weather turned, bringing clouds and rain. All their equipment developed problems and nothing worked. Their guns jammed, their vehicles wouldn't start, and even their fires wouldn't stay lit. In addition, people started having small accidents and getting sick.

This turn of events caused them to rethink their behavior.

They approached the cliff, apologized to the Elves, took down their targets and cleaned up and moved the latrine. Immediately afterward, the sun came out, things started working again, people started feeling better, and the rest of the trip was a success.

It makes perfect sense that Elves would be the dominant nature spirits in Iceland.

This is a land of sparse vegetation and almost no wild animals except birds, arctic foxes and rats. Iceland is a place where the mineral kingdom is dominant and prominent, with rocky plains, glaciers, waterfalls, mountains, and 120 volcanoes, 10 of which are active. Elves are the nature spirits that take care of the mineral kingdom, so their prominence in Iceland is understandable.

Nature spirits exist everywhere however, not just in Iceland.

Fairies or plant elementals are responsible for helping plants grow and thrive. Plant devas act as architectural guides and are responsible for the form and structure of individual plant species. Elves take care of the mineral parts of the Earth. Yet most humans in the western world are rarely aware of them.

Why do most Icelanders believe in Elves and have tales to tell about their interactions, while other developed nations scoff at such ideas?

My guess is that Icelanders are much more in sync with nature than people in the rest of the developed world. Icelanders have had to adapt to drastic natural cycles such as everlasting summer days, and no light at all in winter, as well as frequent volcanic episodes.

In the summer Icelanders spend as much time as possible out-doors, hiking, biking, and riding their beautiful Icelandic horses, taking full advantage of the extra light. In winter, they concentrate on social functions and team sports, using interaction with others as a way to compensate for lack of light. But even in winter they are outdoors. There is swimming all year round in their plentiful geothermal hot springs, and night skiing under lights.

Icelanders also have to contend with frequent volcanic eruptions, at least one every ten years or so, sometimes more often. They are also greatly affected by glacial melt due to global warming.

They never know exactly when eruptions will come or how bad they will be. They never know whether a landscape they love and have cared for will be wiped away in a minutes. They've seen farms and whole valleys covered with ash and lava, rivers diverted by flooding from glacial melt, bridges wiped out and glaciers evaporate. They have experienced first hand the impermanence of nature and have chosen to adapt to it. They live close to the land and accept and honor nature, rather than try to control it.

In my own experience, close ties to the land and natural cycles have also led to a deep resonance with nature spirits, as well as a desire and ability to work closely with them.

Setting aside special woodland areas for fairies (they don't like to be bothered by humans), gained their help in growing lush gardens on my very poor soil. Communicating with the energetic representatives of the various wild animal species helped negotiate deals with all the critters wanting to chomp on my gardens.

Synchronizing my energy with storms spirits also seems to have helped us escape the worst of the brutal weather that has been plaguing the United States these last few years (and other regions as well).

When aware of a strong storm heading our way, I merge my energy with that of the storm and float the potential for the storm lessening or going around us. The storm can adopt the potential or not, depending on what's best for all. It is not up to me to control the weather, so I am only allowing the storm spirits to know my preference. But my energetic connection with them makes it more probable that the potentials I float will be implemented.

Working with nature spirits means connecting with them energetically and working together in synergy.

I must be willing to understand their point of view and their responsibilities, and be willing to work within these parameters, never imposing my will when not appropriate. I must be open to communication from them when I need to redirect my own course, or pay attention to something I have overlooked. It is a partnership where each side respects and honors the other.

It's not necessary to physically see or hear nature spirits to work with them.

The first step is an awareness of the vast beauty and complexity of the unseen energetic world around us. As more people learn about energy and energetic communication, the more we will increase our ability to communicate and partner with all parts of nature.

For now, however, we can all start with simple feelings of gratitude that honor the role nature spirits play in organizing and maintaining our physical world.

50

Soul to the Rescue

Like many people, I hate going to the dentist. I am traumatized by even the thought of going to into a dentist's office. It is therefore really important for me to have a dentist I know, like and trust.

Which is why I have, for many years, had regular cleanings at my periodontist office, since I do know, like and trust him. On the other hand, I have avoided my regular dental office because every time I go there, a new dentist greets me, (and their prices for cleanings are much higher than the periodontist).

But my periodontist said it was time for new x-rays and the insurance would only pay for those at the regular dentist, so I had to go back.

At this visit, the x-rays were accompanied by a

regular check-up, which I thought perfectly appropriate since I hadn't been back in such a long time. I was having no noticeable problems with my teeth and the x-rays seemed fine, so I expected no bad news.

Imagine my shock and horror when yet another new dentist announced that upon examination, he had discovered I needed two crowns replaced because of decay under them, and one new crown due to a crack in the tooth. The total cost would be over $4,000.00.

The amount of work and the expense were bad enough, but the thought of having this work done by someone I didn't know or trust was even worse. I had often thought of finding a new dentist, but the amount of work this would take and the uncertainty about yet another new person was daunting. I would have to pick from those dentists that take our specific kind of insurance, which ruled out most that might be recommended by friends.

This meant that I would have to pick a dentist solely by calling many dentists and asking questions about what I needed and wanted in a dentist, which, of course, would not necessarily guarantee that I would find the right person. It also meant a lot of work, calling each dentist, weeding out those that didn't meet my criteria and then deciding who was right.

So I dithered, not being able to decide what to do.

Then a few days after my visit, one of my teeth started hurting badly. I naturally thought it was one of the ones that needed to be worked on, but when I called the dentist back to report the discomfort, I found that this was an entirely new situation and the tooth in question was not one of the ones targeted for repair.

Now I was really upset.

But this new development was apparently just what was needed to make me commit to finding a new dentist. As soon as I made this commitment and started the process, the tooth that was bothering me became pain free (and is still fine).

I went online to find a list of dentists taking my insurance, copied down all the ones in our area, and prepared to start calling. I made a list of all the questions I wanted information about and picked up the phone, prepared for a long day of calling and questioning.

As I took a deep breath and grounded to ready myself for the task, I had the sudden insight that my soul was ready and willing to help me out with this.

I got out my dowsing rod (I could also have used a pendulum or personal kinesiology) and simply went through the list, asking my soul to give me a yes or no answer as to which of these dentists met all my criteria and was right for me.

The answers I got were emphatic and unequivocal. Only three dentists out of the 10 on the list met all of my needs.

Then it occurred to me that I hadn't asked one other important question. Are these dentists taking new patients? Again the answers were clear. Only one of the three was taking new patients.

I was stunned. A job I thought would take many hours had been accomplished in less than 5 minutes!

I called this dentist, asked if he were taking new patients (he was), and also asked all the other questions I had on my original list, (which were all answered positively).

So I made an appointment, but decided to reserve judgment until I had actually met the dentist in person and heard what he had to say. Being traumatized by the thought of even entering a dentist's office leaves me naturally suspicious and even hostile when meeting new dentists, so, despite the recommendation from my soul, this is how I entered his office.

But even with my initial hostility and bad attitude, he completely won me over. He was courteous and non-patronizing, and seemed to appreciate my need to question everything and have every movement explained. He also seemed very conservative in his approach even though he has the latest and greatest in new technology, and seemed quite knowledgeable and eager to explain many new procedures.

I told him that the other dentist had recommended some work, but didn't say what.

Upon examination, he singled out the tooth with the crack and said that it should be repaired because of the danger of breaking, but that it could be easily fixed with a simple filling (no crown), with no problem now or in the future. He found no other concerns.

When I asked specifically about decay under the crowns, he said he saw no evidence of that.

I walked out of his office a happy woman, with a total bill of $188.00 for one small filling (rather than $4,000.00), and even better, a dentist whom I really liked and felt I could trust.

Yea soul! Thank you, thank you, thank you!

51
Sam's Message

On January 11, 2012 our beloved dog Sam, passed away. He had been sick for some months but insisted on living life to the fullest even though his condition was quite serious.

But quite suddenly, he just couldn't do it anymore. He was tired and ready to go.

He died in the morning, and that afternoon I had to deliver something to a town an hour and a half away. On the long drive I started reflecting on Sam, his life and death, and mourning his passing.

I know that animals take on some of their human's issues, and I was afraid that perhaps Sam had gotten sick and died because he had taken on too much. I was angry that pets thought they had to play this role and sacrifice for us, and the more I thought about it, the angrier I got. I realized that grief was certainly fueling my anger, and that there was probably much I didn't understand about it all.

So I decided to connect to my soul and ask about why our pets take on our issues when it is not in their best interest.

As I was trying to get in touch with my soul, I sensed Sam's energy insistently trying to get my attention. As I turned my focus on him, he told me very clearly that I should be talking to him about these matters, and not to my soul or anybody else.

And he had a lot to say.

He said that pets' ability to take on their human's issues and release them through sickness and even death, is not a sacrifice, but rather a service that they gladly provide, not because they have to, but because they want to, because they love us. This is their job. They are good at it, they know they are good at it, and they enjoy doing it.

Begrudging a pet this job is like being angry that a midwife is deprived of her sleep because a laboring mother gives birth in the middle of the night.

He also assured me that pets can take on only those things that are ready to be released but are stuck for some reason. Although they can't interfere with the soul's purpose for itself, they are glad to offer assistance whenever and however they can.

As for death, Sam said pets don't see it as the tragedy we do. They know it is just a part of the circle of life, and that they can reincarnate back into the same family if they want to. Because pets live much shorter lives, it is easier for a pet to reincarnate back into a human's life than the other way around. He told me he definitely wanted to come back, but we needed to give him some time before we started to look for him.

Dogs have a special responsibility when we die. When we cross over, our beloved dogs are there to greet us. They are the first to meet us and help us remember we have done this many times before.

Sam also talked about the change in people's relationships to their pets in the last couple of decades. Pets today are more a part of the family, are recognized as important beings in their own right, and are given much more love and attention than previously. As people have become more attached to their pets, pets are able to serve in more and better ways.

"The more you love us, the more you love yourselves, for we are part of you". —Sam

52

Digital SoulSpeak

Your soul is always with you, and always trying to communicate.

Here's an example from my life.

I am a writer, so I am often sending book proposals out to publishers. This is a process accompanied by anxiety and nail biting, since there are many components to a book proposal and each has to be carefully crafted and individualized to fit the publisher you are sending it to. It is almost more work than writing the book in the first place, especially since there is no guarantee a publisher will even read your proposal, let alone publish your book.

One Friday, I had a proposal ready to go. I had a "thumbs up" from my writing coach, all the components of my proposal reviewed and edited, and had everything proof-read 40 thousand times. I very carefully got everything formatted for my first email submission and clicked on "send".

OH NO! An error message!

The email wouldn't send! To make things even worse, the whole email, attachments and all, was swallowed by the computer. It wasn't even saved in "drafts". It was gone!!! How could this have happened?

So I tried sending myself a test email and that wouldn't work either. My email was frozen.

The error message was not one I understood. I didn't know what to do.

After having the normal meltdown that anyone would have in a situation like this, I remembered to pull my energy back to me and ground.

Then I began to wonder if there was more to this than just a computer problem. The more I stayed in this quiet place and felt into the energy of the situation, the more I was certain that there was important information here for me.

I decided to ask my soul what was going on. I got out my dowsing rod (I could have used a pendulum or any personal kinesiology technique as well, or just felt into it more), and asked if there was something I should know. The answer was yes. Then I asked if there was something wrong with the proposal. The answer was no. Then I asked if there was something wrong with the timing. The answer was yes.

I grounded again and a light bulb went off in my head. The day was Friday, probably a very bad day to try to get anyone's attention via email. So I asked whether my email froze because today was Friday, and not a good time to send submissions. The answer was yes. Then I asked if Monday was the day I should send things out. The answer was also yes.

A few seconds later my email unfroze, and has been fine ever since.

On Monday morning, I successfully submitted proposals to all chosen publishers with no problems.

Morals to the story:
1. Computers are very energy sensitive, and thus good conduits for soul communication.
2. Bad things are often good things in disguise.

Section Eleven

The Larger World

53
Political Chaos

We certainly seem to be in a crisis of governance, not only here in the United States, but all over the world.

While people struggle to find jobs to support themselves and their families, the financial and political elite insist on austerity for just those struggling people. This, of course, just leads to more job loss and misery, with few, other than millionaires, able to pay the increased taxes needed to keep government solvent.

But instead of paying taxes, the elite want tax cuts for themselves, and many of them would also like to dismantle government completely. Then there are equally many who want to ask those who have more, to do more to support government. We have a situation where the two sides seem to be at polar opposites, with neither willing to negotiate or compromise.

Ideally, conservative and progressive energies are both needed for energetic balance.

Conservatives keep progressives from going off the deep end, and progressives keep conservatives from getting stuck in the past. Achieving balance, however, means that both sides have to listen to each other, and have the good of the whole as a goal, rather than the good of their particular group or themselves personally.

In order to understand what's happening, let's first look at the energetic definition of government.

Although the physical world assumes all material objects are separate, the energy realm is rooted in wholeness and connection.

Every individual cell, organism, person, county, state, or nation is not just an entity unto itself, but also a part of a larger whole. And these wholes are not only defined by the sum of their parts, but also by the number and kind of relationships between and among them.

There are millions of cells in the human body, but even though they can each be separated and identified as individuals, the number and kind of relationships between them (and the larger whole), will determine whether the organism they are a part of is healthy or diseased. If a number of cells decide to alter or sever these relationships so that they are

It's All About Energy: Adventures in Expanded Reality

no longer serving the whole, the result is cancer or some other serious disease that can endanger the life of that organism.

Whether we like to admit it or not, individual humans are also a part of a larger whole.

No matter how self-sufficient we try to be, almost all of us (particularly today in our highly technological culture) are dependent upon relationships that connect us to the the larger world.

Not only our very survival, but also our social and family connections, our food and livelihoods, our ability to travel and communicate, and everything that makes life more comfortable and interesting are dependent on these connections.

In our wisdom as a human species, we have invariably formed governments to set up the structure of relationships we need to survive and thrive. We call these connections "infrastructure" and then forget about them.

The governmental infrastructure consists of defense, roads and bridges, airports and air tower controllers, food and drug safety, laws and justice, telecommunications, research and development of all kinds, and many more.

We, as a collective, authorize our government to do the things as a collective, that we lack the means to do as individuals. This infrastructure needs energy (money) to function, but many people today have forgotten how dependent we all are on this infrastructure, and do not realize the catastrophe we all would face if government should collapse.

Since we created these relationships we can also dismantle or starve them, as many are trying to do today. But what would happen if we dismantled the relationships between the cells in our bodies?

The infrastructures of our current civilization are ancient. Having distinct socio economic classes, and lines between those with power and authority, and those without, used to serve the whole because not everyone had the time or the ability to acquire the resources or knowledge necessary to run the government. Just like the mini-cultures portrayed in Downton Abbey, everyone knew their place and worked hard to serve the whole in whatever capacity they found themselves.

With the advent of the internet and global instant communication, however, these divisions are no longer necessary. In the 21st century, power and authority lie in knowledge and information, which is increasingly available to everyone for much less time and effort than ever before.

At the same time, we are beginning to understand that while we are citizens of an individual country, we are also citizens of the global community.

Our governmental infrastructure needs to become increasingly interactive, co-creative and collaborative, with active participation from the collective, not just in voting but also in knowledge and idea sharing.

In this way we can truly profit from the diverse experiences of the entire population, as well as our connections to those in other nations and parts of the globe. At the same time, each national government must work together with other nations for the good of the planet.

The natural state of energy is balance, so high energy will always gravitate to fill spaces with low or no energy.

Right now, the energy state of the world is quite unbalanced, with those controlling much of the monetary energy preventing it from flowing to lower states. Once elites have accumulated a lot of energy (money), they stop its natural flow by taking advantage of tax loopholes, legal and political manipulation and offshore tax havens.

Ironically, preventing flow to the larger population will also prevent more energy (money) from flowing to the person or institutions hoarding it. And forcing austerity on those who have no or low energy in the first place, will only increase the unbalance and speed up the inevitable breakdown of the whole.

And this is exactly what is happening. What we are witnessing is duality in its extreme.

Absolute opposition, however, is one of the prerequisites for an increase in conscious awareness. Extreme polarity forces us to pay attention to things we may have been unconscious of before.

Beverly Crane, PhD.

A large percentage of everyday people are already beginning to realize the power they have and are starting to exercise it.

They're exercising it by using their cell phones to document police violence. They're organizing and joining demonstrations, and pouring into congressional town hall meetings to let their elected representatives know how they feel. They're blogging and tweeting their ideas and opinions about everything. People from all over the world are collaborating and crowdsourcing to solve problems.

The ancient infrastructural relationships are disintegrating, and their replacements only just beginning to be thought out. The chaos we are seeing in our political centers is a result of these changing infrastructural needs that are a direct result of an evolving human consciousness.

Seeing things as energy can better help us understand what is happening currently in the world as well as how best to solve our problems in the future.

Where we go from here is up to us, but it's not as bleak as it seems. All is well in all creation because things are evolving for the good of all.

54

Recording Revolution

Did you ever stop to think about the remarkable changes that are resulting from the fact that millions of people now carry instant recording devices around in their pockets all the time?

Cell phone cameras record police brutality in a way that leaves little defense for the perpetrators. The gang rape of a woman in India brings instant global condemnation. YouTube has hundreds of videos of political gaffs and incredibly stupid statements from politicians on all sides and levels of government.

Loaded, inaccurate and even false statements meant to rally supporters now go viral, exposing hidden agendas, and institutional and personal deceit. Instant digital access allowed Manning and Snowden, both comparatively low level operators, to spirit away and expose thousands of secret documents about what the US government is doing at taxpayer's expense.

Since Snowden, we are also becoming concerned about the government invading our personal privacy, which in the United States is guaranteed by the Constitution.

Ironically, the government is spying on us, in part, because we are spying on them. And this baby is not going back in the box.

Our technology is allowing us to overturn all the rocks and expose the vermin beneath. It's not that all this nasty stuff wasn't happening before. It's just that in the past we didn't know about it, or chose not to acknowledge it if we did.

Human beings are now ready to let in more light. We are ready to be more honest with ourselves and take responsibility for our actions. We're OK with posting silly pictures of ourselves on Facebook because we know we are just being human.

Along with our willingness to take responsibility and be more honest with ourselves, however, we are also demanding that others be more honest with us.

We want to be fully informed about what the government is doing so we can know what we are voting for. We want to be in control of our personal information, and who gets to use it and why. And so our technology has evolved to allow us to shine the light where there was darkness before.

With the advent of cellphones and instant electronic data transfer, it is becoming harder and harder to be a hypocrite, tell a lie, bribe someone, hide your true feelings, cheat at anything, treat people unfairly, lie or keep secrets. We are just beginning the discussion about what is legitimate or illegitimate personal data collection, and how much control we should have over our own personal information.

We seem much more willing than past generations to share personal information, but only with explicit permission. And in return, we expect transparency and fairness from those we deal with, including, and especially, our government officials and the corporations we buy our stuff from.

It is not surprising that governments are fighting back and cracking down. It is not surprising that politicians are getting caught with their pants down and their feet in their mouths. It is not surprising that corporations are buying politicians and votes. It is not surprising that police are confiscating camera phones, and arresting those that try to document incidents.

The powers that be are scared, and they should be. The cat is already out of the bag and long gone.

Because of the power of that instant recording device and its silicon chip brothers, we have the ability to demand honesty and accountability from both the people and the institutions around us. And we are beginning to accept the responsibility that this power brings.

We are all in this together, and together we can build a fairer, brighter, more honest and peaceful world.

55

Adjusting to Changing Energy

After returning from a recent overseas trip, I felt disoriented and distracted.

It was difficult, if not impossible, to get back into the groove of things as they were before. It was as if the groove had completely disappeared. I felt like my energy field has been blasted to bits, and I had to pick up the pieces and rearrange them in a way that was somehow more comfortable.

Traveling is always expansive, and reorientation does take time. But traveling in the last few years seems different from returning from earlier trips. Lately I have definitely felt like the person I was when I left home, was not the person who returned.

So it's not just the travel. Something else is going on.

That something else is the changing energy of the planet. Since 2012, we have been experiencing the clearing needed for new energy to enter and bring new potentials. The Earth is under reconstruction.

Where exactly we are in the process, I don't know, but it certainly seems that the pace of change has quickened lately, and this intensifying energy is drastically affecting everything, from global affairs, to my own personal energy field.

Change is messy and chaotic, but it is not necessarily bad. Think of a remodeling project. (Just the thought makes me cringe.) Think of the destruction that has to take place before the real work can even begin - tearing out walls and windows, ripping up floors or carpets, and throwing out and carting away all the debris. What a mess!

There is some grief as well.

The old space holds wonderful memories, and we've grown comfortable with it even though it no longer fits our needs. So there can be sadness at loss, and resentment at all the chaos and confusion around us. The disruption of our space also affects our energy fields which need to reorient and adapt as well, making us feel even more disconnected and uncomfortable.

After the destructive phase, the actual remodeling can begin.

However this stage is messy too – lots of dust and

dirt, constant hammering and sawing and the inability to use the space that we have taken for granted in the past. But at least we can begin to imagine what it will look like at the end of the process.

This is the difference between a remodeling project and the changes happening on Earth today.

In a remodeling project, we know what the outcome will be and happily anticipate it. That hope and excitement keeps our hearts open to the process, and helps us tolerate the mess and accommodate to the disruption the project creates. The more open and positive our energy, the more able we are to manifest the potentials that help the project turn out well, even if there are unexpected twists and turns along the way.

After 2012, the Earth, with humanity's permission, began its remodeling project. Looking at world affairs today, it seems like we are still in the destructive stage, but who knows! It's all messy.

Change without a clear vision of outcome produces fear, anger and resentment in many. When confronted with chaos and confusion it is easy to expect the worst, rather than anticipate the best. These negative emotions are full of friction and separate us from the potentials needed for a positive outcome. They interfere with the process of change in the same way getting angry with your contractor would slow and complicate the remodeling project.

The changes we are experiencing will take a while. There is obviously much to do. And even after they're completed, there is the reorganization that must take place after every reconstruction project is finished.

This reconstruction project will move us into an energy reality where nothing stands still. In other words, stasis is no longer possible. We will never go back to "normal". Energy is in constant motion, and as we move into a new world that recognizes energy reality, our lives will be in constant motion as well.

What can we do to take care of ourselves?

1. Breathe. When fear and doubt raise their heads, take a moment to do some deep breathing, bringing your energy back to you in order to release any interference from outside influences.

    If that doesn't do it, breathe your energy down into the ground (grounding) and ask the Earth to help smooth out any residual roughness or friction. Keep breathing until the fear has passed, and your connection with Earth energy has helped you regain trust in the process.

2. Open your heart. Greet the process with an open heart and a flexible mind, no matter how messy and chaotic life seems at the moment.

    Our openness allows connection to the

highest potentials and facilitates their actualization. We don't even have to know what the potentials are since our openness to them will automatically bring the best forward. Openness and flexibility allow us to move gracefully through change.

3. Accept and appreciate. Love and accept ourselves just as we are.

   Choose connection and appreciation over separation and intolerance. Fear, and its siblings, frustration, anger, doubt and resentment, cause friction, throw monkey wrenches into the construction process, and block connection to positive potentials. Love and appreciation facilitate harmony and creative synergy. In this way we become facilitators of evolution rather than victims.

4. Dream large. Dreaming is the way potentials are born.

When we add our individual dreams to the collective vision, we float those potentials for others to pick up, encouraging and supporting their actualization. In this way, we can all be co-creators in the next phase of the process. Our dreams of today are the realities of tomorrow.

56

What Does Freedom Mean?

Well, that's a dumb question. Most of us think we know the answer without even thinking.

Freedom means not being restrained physically and able to make decisions for ourselves without coercion from outside sources. As long as we are not incarcerated or overtly coerced, we probably think we're free.

But the definition of freedom in modern life is much more complicated.

Most of us are not as free as we think. Today true freedom is defined not so much by lack of overt physical restraint and coercion, as it is by awareness of all the covert mental, emotional and energetic manipulation bombarding us every day.

Awareness is meta-consciousness, that is, being conscious of being conscious. Living in an expanded reality means expanding our consciousness with new awarenesses whenever possible. Expanded reality can't be achieved without an expanded awareness regarding the many sophisticated means of manipulating our thinking.

When I was in high school not long after the McCarthy era, the good legislators of my state decided every high school student should be subjected to a semester-long course entitled "Communism vs Democracy".

Can you imagine the dismay of the poor teachers who were tapped to teach this course on barely a moment's notice with no background or time to come up with a meaningful curriculum?

I lucked out, however. My teacher was a veritable genius. She decided to use this course to raise our awareness, and teach us about the real meaning of freedom.

Since one of the most pejorative things about Communism at the time was its propaganda, my teacher took the opportunity to teach us about all the ways propaganda is used, not just in the Soviet Union, but also right here on our doorstep.

She taught us about advertising and the subtle way it manipulates our thinking and gets us to do its bidding even when we think we are making our own decisions. She taught us about public relations, public speaking and speech writing, and how the right words can sway people emotionally without resorting to any kind of logic or facts.

When we buy things, it is important to ask ourselves why we are buying this and not that, or why we are buying in the first place. Has an ad tugged us emotionally so we somehow feel more validated, successful or superior because we own this product? How do we know that the product even works? What about its environmental impact? Think of all the money we women spend on beauty products!

She taught us how our ego's desire for fame and fortune make celebrities far more influential than they ought to be. Subconsciously we think that by paying attention to them, we can somehow draw their energy and success to us, and make it our own. We automatically assume that doing what they recommend, or buying what they tell us to buy, will make that connection stronger and more likely to bring results.

That is why we are drawn to celebrities. That is why celebrity endorsements are big money makers for companies. Celebrities are the ultimate manipulators, but we eat it up anyway without realizing our egos are betraying us.

My teacher also taught us how easy it is to confuse correlation with causation, and how people try to use this confusion to color our thinking.

Correlation is a statistical name for association. In experimentation, if two elements are correlated it means they appear together. But even though that may suggest that one causes the other, this may not be the case at all, and further experimentation needs to be done to find out.

Nonetheless, association has an extremely strong psychological influence on our thinking and emotions.

Symbols and metaphors are all about association. They are effective because they work deep in our sub-conscious on our emotions rather than our logic. This is why art, poetry and dreams are full of associative language and images. This is why commercials and political ads are full of subtle and not so subtle associations. My teacher taught us how certain words and images used together can grab the ego and the emotions to ensure a particular response.

When the FBI director announced that Hillary Clinton had emails on Anthony Wiener's computer, just the association of Hillary with a known pedophile was catastrophic. More emails would have been bad enough, but emails on Wiener's computer were deadly, subtly implying that Hillary must be a pedophile too!

Politicians, advertisers and even charities use association with things we like and things we don't, to influence our behavior even though there may be no factual or causal relationship between the two things associated.

And finally, my teacher taught us about fear, and how those in power, and/or those who want power, use fear to manipulate and dominate.

She taught us to understand how vulnerable we are when we are afraid. Fear takes us back to our childhood, when most of us were protected by our parents. So when we are fearful, even as adults, we automatically look to authority to protect us.

Demagogues, dictators, politicians and bullies of all kind know this instinctively. Instead of inspiring people to come together and help themselves, those who want to control find scapegoats and villains so that even more fear can be generated.

When people are fearful, anyone who says they will protect us and seek revenge, is hailed as a savior. The more fearful people are, the more power the "protector" is given. The more power he is given, the more control he has. The more control he has, the more dangerous he becomes.

Whenever we make a decision based on fear, we are voluntarily giving up our freedom. When we are afraid, we give away our energy to anyone we think might help. Then we become even more vulnerable and powerless.

The next time you find yourself fearful, remember to take some deep breaths, and pull your own energy back to you.

I'm always surprised at how much better I feel after doing this. When I consciously reclaim my own energy, things are no longer hopeless, and I find strength and optimism that definitely wasn't there before. Things that were murky become clear. Once again, I feel confident making my own decisions, and having my own opinions, even if they are different from others around me. Solutions and insights may also pop into my head seemingly out of the blue.

Today there are many people, institutions, organizations, individuals, corporations and even charities who are guilty of using fear to try to make us do things we might not do otherwise.

Let's not go there.

Energy is power. When we feel fearful and powerless it is usually because we have consciously or unconsciously given away our energy.

The ultimate freedom is knowing how to retain and/or reclaim our own personal energy so that we are not susceptible to covert manipulation, and can think clearly about how to proceed. Freedom is dependent upon our ability to consciously reflect on what is being said and done, and then choose how we respond to it.

All of us are susceptible to covert manipulation if we do not consciously check ourselves and our responses routinely. If we always seek to know whether our response is dependent on an emotional tug, we can detect whether there is subtle pressure being applied, (or whether we may be susceptible to it at a later date).

True freedom exists only when the mind is free. As Nelson Mandala and many other wise people have said, though the body may be in chains, the mind is constrained only when we allow it to be.

Section Twelve
Wrapping It All Up

57
Spiritual Perfection

In the spiritual quest for enlightenment, we will almost automatically strive for perfection.

We think that the closer we get to finding our spiritual source, the closer we get to being "perfect". We think we must eliminate all those parts of us that we don't like, that limit us, that are selfish, ugly, messy and/or socially unacceptable. We think we have to have the perfect body, be in perfect health and all those other things that we think of as perfection.

In thinking this way, we make the mistake of attaching our physical ideals to our spiritual aspirations.

We look at those who seem to have everything: a

beautiful and healthy body, an abundant lifestyle, a successful career, a loving family, as somehow being rewarded for having pleased God.

We ourselves, who are struggling in various aspects of our lives, see ourselves as less worthy, less valuable, less close to the spiritual perfection we long for. And part of the reason we long for spiritual perfection, is the illusion that once attained, all our problems will melt away.

Nothing could be further from the truth.

Much anguish about our problems stems from the false belief that the presence of problems in our lives means that there is something spiritually wrong with us, and consequently we are unworthy and will never attain the enlightenment we seek.

Remember that perfection is an invention of the physical world. Perfection could only happen if, in fact, we lived in a world where stasis was the only reality.

Perfection is stasis. When something is perfect, any change would destroy that perfection. And perfection is different for everyone. Self-imposed beliefs about what is perfection limit our ability to see beyond, to discover potentials that are not yet visible. The idea of perfection stifles and confines us.

Perfection means always being successful, never making a mistake, and never breaking the bonds of that self-imposed prison.

It is only by failing, by facing limitations and by making mistakes, that we break out, widen our horizons and find new opportunities. Perfection is impossible in a world where flow is the norm. Perfection and transformation cannot exist together.

When we are hungry, we are willing to try foods we would never have tried before. When we fail, we are offered new and important information about how to reach our goals. When we make mistakes, they are opportunities to expand our horizons.

Expanding our reality helps us realize that perfection is an illusion.

Even in physical reality, the most perfect creation can always be improved upon. The evolution of the human species depends on the continuous flow of energy that cannot stay still, no matter what. We need look no further than the rapid flow of technology today for proof of this claim.

No matter what our supposed "problems", they are here to serve us; to move us forward, to test our ingenuity, to guide us to opportunities we wouldn't have encountered if we had not had to solve the challenges in our lives.

There is no such thing as spiritual perfection because we never stop growing and experiencing all of creation as creative beings. We never stop wanting and needing to experience the life events that help us gather wisdom and compassion.

Expanding into the energy dimension doesn't mean that our problems will vanish. But it does mean we can tackle them with an entirely different attitude.

When we see them from a soul perspective, with knowledge of the energetic rules that govern them, we no longer judge ourselves and others harshly, we are excited by the challenges they bring, and we know there is a solution even if we don't know what it is at the moment.

We realize that spiritual enlightenment has nothing to do with not having problems, but everything to do with how we look at them.

There is also a tendency to think of unity as part of spiritual perfection, that all our problems here on Earth are the result of this planet's dualistic nature. There is a real yearning by many for a return to a primordial unity where dualism and opposition don't exist.

Remember that dualism is necessary for the growth of conscious, and there is no limit to that growth. In fact, the growth of consciousness through experiences that include opposition is imperative for the continued evolution of both the human species and our individual spiritual lives.

Returning to unity would negate not only duality but diversity. Returning to unity would expunge the glorious variety found in the physical world that delights our senses and sparks our curiosity. Returning to unity would relegate us to huddling in compounds with only those who think and look like we do. Returning to unity would negate the very reason for the creation of the universe, both physical and energetic, in the first place.

The good news is that duality doesn't have to be full of friction, conflict, war and destruction.

As we begin to expand our reality into the energy dimension we can begin to see duality in its purest form, as a necessary vehicle for both physical survival and the growth of consciousness.

In an expanded reality, duality becomes a necessary tool that has both positive and negative elements. It is up to each of us as to which we choose.

We can also begin to see unity in an entirely different light, that is, as the human ability to reconnect, to bring things together, to organize disparate elements into a synergistic whole, rather than a retreat to primal oneness.

The ability to see the larger picture, to understand connections and create a whole out of supposedly unrelated elements is a gift that only humans possess. The ability to unify is part of our creative nature, and the very essence of the human soul.

58

Integrating the Realms

Once you start to understand how it all fits together, integrating the realms is not difficult.

We will always be most comfortable in the 4D realm of physical reality, so the biggest challenge is remembering that we can expand, that we have other choices as to how we see things, and other choices as to how we act and react.

How do we remember?

We are able to remember the existence of the energy dimension any time we choose to think about it. We remember when we go into meditation. We remember when we participate in an inspiring moment, a walk in the woods, an intimate exchange with a loved one, a sudden intuitive "hit".

It gets harder when we become enmeshed in day to day problems and struggles.

This is when it is really important to remember, but also when we are least likely to do it. The energies of frustration, anger, rage, despair, and conflict are full of friction and incoherence. This kind energy disrupts our fields and makes returning to coherence and synergy quite difficult. Even if we remember that there is another way, regaining balance and trust is not easy. Until we learn to manage our own energy, we will not be able to make the shift.

This is when it is important to make conscious choices and use energetic tools. We have lived in a limited 4D world all our lives, so moving beyond those limits takes time and practice.

I like to use a common mnemonic device to help. This device is simply the beginning of the alphabet, ABCD and E.

A is for Awareness. Before changing your perspective, you have to remember, to become aware that there are other options. This is perhaps the hardest part of the process, but once you become aware, it is much easier to remember the rest of the sequence.

B is for Breath, remembering to breathe your energy back to you. Just breathing has a calming effect and helps the body regain the balance and coherence lost. (Recall that your mother always told you to take 3 deep breaths whenever responding to a traumatic, upsetting or aggressive encounter.) Consciously pulling your energy back to you with your breath, removes it from the toxic effects of people or circumstances around you.

C is for Center. Once you have pulled your energy back to you, return it to your center where you have control over it. Now you can make a choice as to how you want to manage it. C also stands for Choice.

Sometimes just taking some deep breaths and remembering your options will be all you need. But again, regaining coherence after an onslaught of negative energy is not easy. Often just breathing will not be enough.

D is for down. When breathing is not enough, it is helpful to ground, that is, to take your energy down further out through your feet into the Earth. It helps to imagine your energy blending with the energy of the Earth, which is always a source of harmony and coherence.

Energy has a peculiar quality called resonance, which means that energy will tend to equilibrate to any other energy that is larger and more positive. Remember the tuning forks. When they are first struck, they will vibrate with different tones, but after a few seconds the tones will synchronize and vibrate on the same note.

When you ground, your energy is exposed to a vast field of energy that is vibrating with deep harmony and resonance with the universal field. This means that imagining your own energy blending with Earth energy will bring harmony and balance back to you. Keep breathing down until you feel coherence return.

Synchronizing your energy field to the universal field by grounding, also creates a direct connection to universal wisdom that can often provide important intuitive information.

Grounding both connects you to the source of wisdom and also provides the physical structure (ground into matter) that organizes information into a form that is recognizable by human consciousness.

Many stories in this book have demonstrated how grounding in the middle of frustration, panic or upset can bring amazing and miraculous insights.

Here's one more example.

Many years ago, when my children were young, my husband invited the family to go with him to a conference held in an upscale hotel in a distant city. He felt the children would love a chance to use the large swimming facility and ride the glassed-in elevators up 10 stories overlooking the gardens beneath.

The trip was a big success, and all of us piled into

our van at noon on Saturday when the conference was over. After turning the key to start the van, it was obvious that something was very wrong with the transmission. Strangely, neither my husband nor I panicked. We just looked at each other and he said, "I'll get the mechanic and tow truck", and I said, "I'll find a rental car".

In just a short time, he had accomplished his tasks and the tow truck was on its way.

I, on the other hand, could not find a rental car in all of the city. They either wouldn't answer the phone, were out of cars, or did not deliver to our location. Soon the tow truck arrived and took the van and my husband off to the repair shop.

Left alone in a strange city with two small children and no rental car, I panicked and almost lost it. Only the thought of my children caused me to pause and think about my options. I then realized how out-of-control I was, and how much I needed to use my energetic tools. I took some deep breaths, pulled my energy in, and grounded.

Not only did I feel better immediately, I was also hit with a strong intuitive certainty that the reason I couldn't find a rental car was because I wouldn't need one. The van would be fixed in time for us to make it home that evening!

This certainty was obviously not logical. What are the chances of getting a transmission fixed on Saturday afternoon in a strange city?

Yet I knew it was true.

It's All About Energy: Adventures in Expanded Reality

I piled the kids into the hotel's limousine, gave the address of the repair shop, and a short while later we arrived just as the mechanic was finishing his examination of the van.

"Good news", he said. "It's not the transmission, it's the transmission cable. Even though it's Saturday, I have a key to the warehouse and will send a man right over to get the part. Oh, and here's the key to my car, go have fun and come back at four. It will be done by then."

And it was.

I have had many other experiences like this one, but only if I remember to pull my energy back and ground. This skill has certainly made life much easier, and I have been able to save much time, effort, frustration and a lot of hassles because of it.

And finally, E is for energy. Once your energy is grounded, connected and coherent, you can ask it to serve you. This is when you can set your intentions, when you can put in motion the synchronicities and energy movement needed to make your dreams reality.

In order to help you visualize the processes described here I have included two guided visualizations in the Appendix. The first one, called Running Energy, takes you through the first four steps (ABCD) described in this chapter. The second deals with E, and will be explained in the next chapter.

59

How to Enter the Flow

The key to living in both realms at the same time is learning how to access the flow.

Entering the flow means synchronizing your energy field to that of the universal energy flow so that energy can naturally work for you. It means allowing (and trusting) energy to serve you rather than fighting circumstances and trying to control everything that happens to you.

Life in the physical realm has taught us that control is everything. When bad things happen, we store them away in our memories, determined to learn from them and avoid any situation that is similar. We are constantly scanning our environment for red flags so we can protect ourselves. Most of the time, our due diligence pays off.

We observe the dangers in our physical environment so we can avoid them. We buy insurance to protect against health problems or natural disasters. We have auto insurance to protect us from the medical and legal problems that might result from an accident. Planning ahead for possible risks does make our life easier and less anxiety ridden.

Entering the flow does not mean we cease doing these things. Living in both realms at the same time means taking advantage of whatever means are at our disposal for minimizing possible problems in the future.

There are some things we cannot control however, some things we cannot foresee. This is where entering the flow comes in. This is why entering the flow takes trust and courage.

Giving up control is not easy, so we tend to grab on and resist when we think things are not going the way we want them to. It takes trust in the process and a willingness to let go.

Letting go of that resistance is what allows energy to start working for you.

Entering the flow is about choice. When you are faced with a situation you can't control, you can choose to enter the flow and trust that whatever happens will be in your best interest . . . . or you can resist.

The importance of making this conscious choice

was brought home to me some time ago (before cell phones and their time keeping ability), when my watched stopped working. I assumed it needed a new battery and put it on the kitchen table to remind me to take it to town. But on Monday morning I went off and left it, much to my dismay.

I needed my watch, so at first I was upset. I had only a short time between many appointments and knew that going home to get it would cause me to be late and stressed out. Even if I did go home and get it, I would then not have time to go to the store to get a battery.

When I realized there were no good options, I knew I had a choice. I could resist and let my lapse of memory ruin my whole day, or I could find a way to enter the flow and trust that everything would be fine. I chose to enter the flow.

It was only then I remembered the many problems with my watch. Although I really liked the watch, it was old and the gold plating was coming off. My skin was sensitive to the metal underneath causing me to have to remove it at night. Sweat also reacted badly with the metal so I could not wear it during exercise or physical work without developing a rash.

These thoughts came in a flash, and along with them, the realization that it was a new watch I needed, not a new battery! And I had just enough time between appointments to go to the store and pick out exactly what I wanted.

What started as irritation and self-recrimination became a fun process and an opportunity to meet a need I was not even aware I had.

Life presents us with opportunities to enter the flow all the time. Any time we find ourselves frustrated because there is no way to control the situation, we can choose to let go and enter the flow.

We can also choose to start each day by entering the flow for the entire day.

This process has had some really amazing results in my own life, from emerging unscathed from dangerous accident scenes, to large falling trees missing the house by inches with no damage, to finding good parking spaces and all green lights.

Setting your intention to enter the flow for the entire day is a simple process. It involves the ABCDE sequence outlined in the last chapter, except this time, after going through the sequence, you concentrate on the E.

Once you have pulled your energy back to you, centered and grounded, you are free to place that energy wherever you want it.

First you bring that newly harmonized and purified energy back up through your body and place it where you need it.

You can place it in your root chakra (at the bottom of your torso) for strength and stability when for example, you are trying to open a jar, or asking your boss for a raise. You can place it in your second chakra (just below the navel) when you want to have good sex.

Placing it in your third chakra, (beneath the sternum) is good for issues of willpower, self-confidence and personal identity.

The heart or fourth chakra is where you place your energy when dealing with other people, when you want to access compassion and understanding, and especially when extending blessings.

Extra coherent energy in the fifth or throat chakra will help with all kinds of communication, from giving a speech, to articulating a point, to negotiating a disagreement with wisdom and respect for the other's position.

The sixth chakra, or third eye, can be helpful for solving problems and getting intuitive insights, and the crown chakra facilitates connection with your soul and accessing energy from Source.

You can also choose to place your energy in many places depending on the situation. For example, when asking for a raise, you could place your energy in your first chakra for strength and stability, in your third chakra for self-confidence, in your fourth chakra for connection and compassion, and in your fifth chakra for finding just the right words. Your energy can be anywhere you choose for it to be, and in many places at the same time.

It's All About Energy: Adventures in Expanded Reality

Choosing where we place harmonized and coherent energy can have remarkable effects on our everyday tasks.

When choosing to enter the flow, however, we bring that energy up through the crown or seventh chakra to a place about a hand's length from the top of our head. This is the soul chakra, and the symbolic door to the energy realm. Imagine a fine, invisible veil in this space that separates the physical from the energetic, then gently part the curtain and step through.

In this space, you have access to both the physical realm and the energetic realm. Setting an intention to enter the flow for the entire day, and then parting the curtain and stepping through, is a meaningful ritual that will greatly affect your whole day.

The second guided imagery in the Appendix is a step-by-step guide as to how to do this.

60

A Time of Transformation

Even though we are living in turbulent times, there are great opportunities. Turbulence and chaos carry huge potentials for transformation.

As more and more institutions and situations disintegrate into dysfunction, more and more energy is freed up. Rather than being locked away in fully functional, self-sustaining systems, this energy is now liberated, just waiting to be channeled into creative, compassionate, sustainable solutions to our many problems.

This new energy won't automatically solve problems, however. It has to be guided, directed and formed by human consciousness.

Now that you are familiar with the energy realm and how to engage with it, you can help.

The first step is the formation of ideas and goals. Freed up energy needs to be organized, that is, given shape and purpose. This step is something we all can do. While creation with matter needs tools, resources and physical labor, creating with energy needs only imagination and intention.

The second step involves physical actions where those imaginative solutions and visions are actually brought into physical reality by those who have the training and resources to do so. But the ideas have to come first, so that those with training and resources don't have to do the whole job. Instead, they can simply grab a floating potential that is already out there just waiting to be worked with, and begin to make it a reality.

If you would like to be part of this grand transformational process, sit back, take some deep breaths, relax completely and prepare to engage your imagination and creativity.

Close your eyes and begin to imagine a bright green and blue Earth, where the sea, air and land are free from pollution, where the creation of physical goods takes into consideration sustainability and recycling at the end of their life, where our world economic system is based on fair energy exchange and openness, rather than greed and deceit, where people and nations feuding for centuries, lay down their swords and clasp hands, where governments are designed for the good of all citizens and run by committed public servants who realize that we are all connected, and what benefits all, will also bring most benefit to them personally.

Don't worry about the details of your vision. The details can't be filled in until the larger vision is formed.

Allow yourself to imagine a place where the justice system is designed around compassion, understanding and reintegration into society, rather than punishment, retribution and condemnation, where beauty and the arts are acknowledged as the soul's expression, are financially sustained and seen as a means of exploring new ideas and potentials, where creators and inventors openly share ideas, knowing that co-creation, collaboration and crowdsourcing are a faster, surer and more efficient way of solving problems than competition, hoarding and trade secrets.

Let your imagination roam to any other part of life here on Earth that is important to you, transforming it into a place of wonder and beauty, honor and compassion.

And when you have transformed all you can think of, prepare to move these potentials you have created into orbit around our Earth.

Imagine that there is an energy cord connecting you in your chair on Earth to a you that exists in the transformed world you have envisioned. Let yourself travel along that cord to the you on the new Earth you have imagined, and then spend a few minutes basking in the world you have created.

Take in the beauty and light, hear the new sounds and vibrations of harmony, smell the fresh smells and taste the wonderful food and water. Feel the honor and respect humans have for one another and their deep connection to the land, the plants and the animals. Let your imagination take flight and experience this new place to its fullest.

Now with simple intention, begin to move this new Earth dimension you have just experienced closer and closer to old Earth, so that the new Earth dimension is superimposed over the old Earth.

Use no force here. Just position this new dimension above the old, but do not attempt to force it upon anyone. Its closeness, just above the heads of all humans on Earth, will offer them the invitation to reach up and take hold of some, or even all of our collective vision, whatever potentials appeal to them.

Some will accept the invitation, and many won't.

Of those who do, some may be in the position to make these ideas reality, but many may just hold them in their imagination, increasing the potential that others will feel that energy and want to accept the invitation as well.

Only a surprisingly small percentage of all people on Earth need to participate in order to effect change.

That was pretty easy, wasn't it?

Now that you're experienced, this next suggestion won't be so difficult. This time imagine the reality you personally would like to live in.

Don't be afraid to dream large. Think about your relationships, your abundance, your health and all those other things that managing your energy field could influence. Floating these potential like you did for the new Earth means they are there for you when and if, you want to choose them.

By floating them right over your head you increase the probability that you will reach out and choose them when you're ready. Learning to manage your energy field and access the energy dimension increases the probability that you will feel comfortable embracing them.

You can repeat these experiences as often as you wish, each time bringing more and more of the vision into form and light.

The energy realm is available to all of us. Now that you have some understanding of how it works and what the rules are, you are ready to explore on your own. Remember that we are only just beginning to understand this amazing new aspect of reality. Each of our personal explorations will bring more information that will benefit everyone.

Be bold. Go explore, then be prepared for further adventures in the mystical, the magical and the miraculous.

Appendix
Helpful Tools

Visualization #1

Running Energy

This guided imagery is designed to help you learn how to consciously control your own energy field.

When you are ready, find a comfortable position . . . close your eyes and begin to breathe deeply. Become aware of your body and any tension you might be feeling . . . As you breathe deeply, feel that tightness begin to drain away as you allow yourself the luxury of becoming completely relaxed. . .(allow time).

Beginning at the top of your head, notice any tension or discomfort you might have there. . . breathe deeply into that area and as you breathe out, breathe away that tension . . . Now move that feeling of relaxation down your face, softening the muscles around your eyes, your jaw and your throat. . .

Focus your attention now on your neck and shoulders, where so many of us carry such heavy loads... Become aware of the tension caused by the many responsibilities we have all chosen to assume...

As you breathe in, give yourself permission to lift that weight... Breathe it away with each breath out. ..(allow time)...

Now let this feeling of deep relaxation in your shoulders sink down into your arms and upper chest. .. Feel the tension drain down your arms and out your fingers... Your chest feels lighter, and with each breath, becomes more open and expansive...

Continue moving this relaxing energy down your body into your stomach and hips... Feel your body becoming almost fluid, sinking softly into the chair... as the tension flows down your legs... into your feet... and out into the earth where it is recycled and purified... (allow time)...

Now your body is completely relaxed.

Begin to picture your own energy in the form of invisible smoke as it circles around the room or follows your thoughts and emotions as they reach out to other people, situations or ideas... Try to feel into the energy surrounding these different aspects of your life in order to sense their different vibrations or frequencies... (allow time)...

Once you have attained some sense of the different places your energy may be, put out the call to gather all your own personal energy back into you... As you breathe in deeply, picture that energy regrouping and returning to your body through your breath, much like a backward running movie of smoke pouring back down a chimney. . . . Or perhaps you would like to envision a golden net that your awareness throws out to gather your energy back to you. . . (allow time).

As this energy returns, breathe it down your spine until it reaches your center, just below your navel. . . (allow time). Then take most of it even further down through your feet, out into the earth . . . Now breathe out, and feel that energy extending out into the earth. . . like tree roots . . .

Feel the stability and firmness, . . .the rootedness and vital connection, . . .the harmony and coherence . . . (allow time) . . .

With each exhalation, imagine yourself releasing any residual tension or toxins in your body down into your roots and back out into the earth . . . Ask the Earth to help purify and harmonize your energy as you consciously blend your energy with hers . . .(allow time).

When your roots have gone down as far as they can go, . . .and when your body is feeling lighter and more open, . . .reverse the process and begin drawing energy up from the earth . . .This energy is healing and nourishing . . . Feel it gather at the base of your spine and slowly continue flowing up your back. . . smoothing, balancing and healing as it goes. . . . (allow time).

Slowly bring this energy up through your body,

into your heart center ... feel this harmonized energy warming and expanding your heart area ... until it spills over, ... blessing and anointing everyone and everything around you.....(allow time).

Then take that energy on up through your head.. ... and out through your crown... When it gets just above your crown, it meets a clear, brilliant celestial energy coming down from above, and the meeting of the two erupts in a geyser of liquid light which cascades down around you, enveloping you like a cocoon ... wrapping you in a blanket of unconditional love.......

Let yourself bask in this warmth and peace while the light clears and cleanses your mind, harmonizes your emotions, revitalizes your body, ... and integrates your soul....(allow time).

When you have allowed yourself to fully feel the healing, balancing and harmonizing flow of peace and warmth coming from the light, ... silently express your gratitude for this experience, knowing you can return at any time...

Now begin to become aware that it is almost time to return to physical reality ... Slowly begin to focus on your physical body and its immediate surroundings ... Feel your feet on the floor, the temperature of the room, and when you are ready, open your eyes...

Visualization #2

Entering the Energy Dimension

This meditation will allow you to experience one of many ways to enter the energy dimension.

When you are ready, close your eyes and begin clearing your mind of all extraneous thoughts . . . pulling down the garage door of your mind, . . . or turning off your mental TV screen . . . Settle your body in a comfortable position . . . and begin to breathe deeply. . . Knowing you are in a safe place. . . just let the tension drain away as you allow yourself to become completely relaxed. . . remembering the last time you were here. . . . allow your body to remember also. . . On a count backward from 5, let yourself sink deeply into a total relaxation of body, mind and spirit—5 . . . 4 . . . 3 . . . 2 . . . 1.

Now find those places where you may have let your personal energy unconsciously slip away from you . . . and then gently bring it back . . by casting a golden net, or just taking some deep breaths, . . . bringing it all back into your body. . .

As this energy returns to you, breathe it down your spine until it reaches your center. . . then with an out breath, take it down through your feet out into the earth . . . grounding yourself firmly in material reality, into structure and meaning . . . gaining strength and extra resources . . . as you breathe out, feel that energy extending out into the earth. . . giving you serenity and confidence. . . Feel the solidity and firmness, . . . the stability and peaceful vitality . . . (allow time) . . . . .

When you feel firmly rooted and connected, reverse the process and begin drawing your energy up from the earth . . . . Feel this energy gather at the base of your spine and slowly continue flowing up your back, . . . move this energy up your body until it reaches your heart area. . . . . Feel your heart opening and expanding, . . . filling with the energy of gratitude and compassion . . . (allow time) . . .

As energy gathers in your chest, it begins to overflow into your environment, radiating an unconditionally loving connection between you and everything around you. . . . Take a few moments to become completely at home with this feeling, . . . so that you can recapture this moment whenever you need to . . . (allow time).

It is from here that we can enter the energy dimension. . . from the heart center. . . from this place of loving connection . . . the place where the physical and the spiritual meet. . .

The next step is to stop time . . . so if you are ready . . . take a deep breathe, then breathe out slowly and hold it as long as you can . . . notice the stillness . . . the silence . . . the mystery of the place between breaths . . where everything stops . . .

Then breathe in as you lift your energy . . . and your awareness up through your throat, through your crown and out into the space above the top of your head . . . Once your energy is clear of your body, begin to look with your imagination for the place where the curtain of physical reality is thinnest, . . .where you can part the curtain and slip through . . . .

If you would like to explore further, knowing you can come back at any time by merely changing your intention, gently part the curtain and step through . . . (allow time) . . .

Notice the change in energy, the stillness and sense of harmony . . . . . and at the same time a profound connectedness and sense of peace . . . (allow time)

Now pause and check your own personal energy . . . Notice how it has changed . . . Notice that it has probably increased in frequency, bringing with it an increasing sense of possibility, of empowerment, of incredible resonance...

From here it is possible to step into the flow of the universe, to feel connected and in sync with everything... If you wish, you can choose to enter that flow now, and harmonize your energy with the energy of the spheres.... where everything always works for the good of the whole, of which you are an important part... allow time)...

Take a few minutes to get used to this place... knowing you can come back any time... (allow time)

This place is the launch pad, the place from which all transformations begin... the place where you can communicate with your soul and the souls of others... the place where you can rearrange probabilities,... the place where creations begin and solutions are found... the place where you can warp time,... the place from where you can place loving energy when and where it is needed... (allow time)...

(Sending Blessings Variation can be added here.)

Now it is time to become aware that this meditation is almost over.... Giving thanks for your experience and knowing you can come back at any time,

... slowly bring your attention back to your physical body ... as you count from one to five, begin to become aware of the chair or floor under you, the light touch of air on your cheek, the temperature of the room, 1...2...3...4... 5...and when you are ready, open your eyes and stretch your body.

Sending Blessings Variation

If you would like, you can now take a few moments to think of those people or places that could benefit from the resonance you are experiencing in this place... (allow time) ...

If you choose, you may send that resonance to them now ... taking care to attach no agenda, no imperative, no judgment as to how they should use what you send. Empower them to make their own choices the best they can....

Send your blessing with your imagination .. in any form that feels right, ... perhaps a gentle drift of gold dust, ... or a soft, warm breeze, ... or maybe in the form of celestial music .. place your gift of energy now ... whereever you feel it is needed most ...

About the Author

Beverly Crane teaches and writes about personal energy management and the magic of energy reality. For the past 25 years she has worked with private clients and taught seminars and workshops throughout the University of Wisconsin system, and at professional conferences and private venues in the upper Midwest..

The founder of *Transformational Expansion* and a blog called *Multidimensional Living*, she works to raise awareness of the energy dimension and the expanded human potential it offers.

She lives in the middle of a forest in rural Wisconsin with her husband, cat and dog.

www.ingramcontent.com/pod-product-compliance
Lightning Source LLC
Chambersburg PA
CBHW020607300426
44113CB00007B/540